Economy and Virtue

Economy and Virtue

Essays on the Theme of Markets and Morality

EDITED BY DENNIS O'KEEFFE

FOREWORD BY DAVID WILLETTS

iea

The Institute of Economic Affairs

First published in Great Britain in 2004 by
The Institute of Economic Affairs
2 Lord North Street
Westminster
London SW1P 3LB
in association with Profile Books Ltd

A CIP catalogue record for this book is available from the British Library.

ISBN 0 255 36504 7

Many IEA publications are translated into languages other than English or
are reprinted. Permission to translate or to reprint should be sought from the
Director General at the address above.

Typeset in Stone by MacGuru Ltd
info@macguru.org.uk

Printed and bound in Great Britain by Hobbs the Printers

CONTENTS

THE AUTHORS

Christopher Badcock

Christopher Badcock is Reader in Sociology at the London School of Economics and Political Science. Although he is a sociologist by training, Badcock's research interests lie very firmly in the camp of evolutionary psychology and modern Darwinism. He has rejected explanations of human behaviour put forward by the standard social sciences model and advocates an interdisciplinary approach to solving such problems.

He was educated at Maidstone Grammar School and received a BSc in sociology and social anthropology at the LSE, where he also completed his PhD in 1973. After lecturing in sociology at the Polytechnic of the South Bank, he was appointed to the staff of the Department of Sociology in 1974. He was also engaged in a private didactic analysis with Anna Freud until her death in 1982. Between 1981 and 1987 he was managing editor and associate editor of the *British Journal of Sociology*. He is a frequent guest on BBC radio, speaking on evolution, psychology and genetics.

Antony Flew

Antony Flew is an emeritus Professor of Philosophy at the University of Reading. He has produced two books on education: *Power to the Parents: Reversing Educational Decline* (London: Sherwood, 1987); and *Shephard's Warning: Setting Schools Back on Course* (London: Adam Smith Institute, 1994). He has also written pamphlets and/or contributed to books published by the Adam Smith Institute, the Centre for Policy Studies, the Institute of Economic Affairs and the Social Affairs Unit. He co-authored *Spiritual Development and All That Jazz*, published by the Campaign for Real Education in York.

Sean Gabb

Sean Gabb is editor of *Free Life*, the journal of the Libertarian Alliance. He was political and economic adviser to the Slovak prime minister in the early 1990s. In the late 1990s he started up the infamous Candidlist, which forced actual or potential Conservative politicians to spell out their beliefs and intentions vis-à-vis European Monetary Union. At present Dr Gabb teaches Economics and Business at the London Metropolitan University. He is a very well-known broadcaster and celebrated for his mastery of the Internet. He is the author of *Dispatches from a Dying Country* (Hampden Press, 2001).

Peter King

Peter King is Reader in Housing and Social Philosophy in the Department of Public Policy, De Montfort University. His publications include: *Housing, Individuals and the State: the Morality of Government Intervention* (Routledge, 1998; with M. Oxley); *Housing: Who Decides?* (Macmillan, 2000); *Housing Benefits* (Adam Smith Institute, 2000); and *A Social Philosophy of Housing* (Ashgate, 2003).

Israel M. Kirzner

Israel Kirzner received his Bachelor's degree at Brooklyn College, Brooklyn, New York, and his Master's and Doctoral degrees at New York University (where he studied under the late Ludwig von Mises). Since 1957 he has been a faculty member at New York University, holding the title of Professor of Economics since 1968. Professor Kirzner's published works include *The Economic Point of View* (1960); *Competition and Entrepreneurship* (1973); *The Meaning of the Market Process* (1992); and 'Entrepreneurial Discovery and the Competitive Market Process: An Austrian Approach', *Journal of Economic Literature*, March 1997. He is also author of 'The Primacy of Entrepreneurial Discovery', in *The Prime Mover of Progress*, IEA Readings No. 23 (1980), and *How Markets Work: Disequilibrium, Entrepreneurship and Discovery*, IEA Hobart Paper 133 (1997).

David Marsland

David Marsland is Professor of Health Informatics at Brunel University. He is an LSE-trained sociologist who has specialised in the study of youth, welfare and research methods. He is an authority on the reform of policy in the public services. His latest book, *Welfare or Welfare State?*, was published by Macmillan in March 1996. In 1991 he was the first winner of the Thatcher Award for contributions to the analysis of freedom. Professor Marsland has lectured to a wide international audience and is a well-known broadcaster and journalist.

Dennis O' Keeffe

Dennis O'Keeffe is Professor of Social Science at the University of Buckingham and Visiting Fellow at the Institute of Economic Affairs. He is a specialist in the sociology and economics of education and has published widely on matters of social theory and education in British and American journals. His critique of British teacher education, *The Wayward Elite*, was published by the Adam Smith Institute in 1990. His innovative study of truancy, *Truancy in English Secondary Schools*, was published by HMSO in 1994. He also specialises in translating social scientific literature from French. For the IEA he is author of the paper *Political Correctness and Public Finance*, Studies in Education No. 9 (1999).

Arthur A. Shenfield

An economist and barrister at law, the late Arthur Shenfield was born and raised in Cardiff. He obtained first-class honours degrees in economics and law and was a Lord Justice Holker Exhibitioner of Gray's Inn. He was called to the Bar in June 1945 and practised from 1945 to 1955. Earlier, he was assistant editor of the London and Cambridge Economic Service and lecturer in economics at the University of Birmingham, prior to entering public service in 1945 as Deputy Controller, Economic Section of the Central Commission for Germany. He served for two years as economic adviser to the government of Trinidad. In 1955, he gave up practice at the Bar and became Economic Director of the Federation of British Industries, which, in 1964, became the Confederation of British Industry, a position that he occupied for eleven years.

He then commenced a second distinguished career, which was to last for over twenty years, as a visiting professor at various American universities and colleges in faculties of both law and economics. These included the University of Chicago; Temple University; the University of California, Davis; the University of Dallas; Clemson University; the University of Colorado; the University of California, San Diego; Rockford College; and Hillsdale College. In 1972 he was elected President of the Mont Pélerin Society. He is the author of several books and monographs (including *Agenda for a Free Society*, *The Nature of Competition*, *The Political Economy of Tax Avoidance* and *Restrictive Practices in the European Economic Community*) and hundreds of articles.

Walter E. Williams

Walter Williams is John M. Olin Distinguished Professor of Economics at George Mason University, Fairfax, Virginia. In addition, he serves as an Adjunct Professor of Economics at Grove City College in Grove City, Pennsylvania. He has also served on the faculties of Los Angeles City College, California State University Los Angeles, and Temple University in Philadelphia. He is the author of over eighty publications which have appeared in scholarly journals such as *Economic Inquiry*, *American Economic Review*, *Georgia Law Review*, *Journal of Labor Economics*, and *Social Science Quarterly*, as well as in popular publications such as *Newsweek*, *The Freeman*, *National Review*, *Reader's Digest*, *Cato Journal*, and *Policy Review*. Dr Williams serves on the boards of directors of Citizens for a Sound Economy, the Reason Foundation and the Hoover Institution, and on the advisory boards of the IEA, the Landmark Legal Foundation, the Alexis de Tocqueville Institute, the Cato Institute and others.

He has frequently given expert testimony before Congressional committees on public policy issues ranging from labour policy to taxation and spending. He is a member of the Mont Pélerin Society and the American Economic Association.

FOREWORD

This important collection of essays tackles a ubiquitous but pernicious error committed by critics of the market, and occasionally even by its advocates. This is to regard the free market as a necessary evil. Even if people reluctantly concede that it works, they don't think it is good or right or admirable. The economic case for the free market has made enormous progress in the past twenty years, not least thanks to the efforts of the IEA. But we are plagued by the assumption that markets are driven by, and indeed promote, human vices such as greed and selfishness. Until such misconceptions cease to be widespread, the case for free markets will not properly have been won.

The distinguished authors in this volume tackle vigorously these misconceptions about the immorality of the market. They make many important points. The motive of selfishness that is often said to underpin a market economy is not, in any meaningful sense, the same as 'self interest', which in reality is the main motivating factor behind economic decisions. Furthermore, the market economy restrains both selfishness and those who wish to do harm to others. The protection of property rights, together with the requirement for contracting parties to consent to market transactions, means that the potential of evil people to do harm is limited. In an economy that is centrally planned, those motivated by selfishness will not gain from mutually beneficial transactions, but rather from working their way up to a point in the political system at which they become entitled to material goods as 'perquisites'.

As Israel Kirzner points out in Chapter 5, the fact that individuals wish to respond to the opportunity for profit – which is a signal that value can be added by combining factors of production in a particular way to provide a product or service – tells us nothing about their moral outlook. And it certainly tells us nothing about their deepest motives. To have more information about their moral outlook we need knowledge of what they did with the profits. Did they donate them to charity? Did they use them to set up a hospice? Did they give a bonus to their employees?

We do, in fact, know that entrepreneurs are motivated by a whole range of subjective desires, but even where profits are used to achieve purely materialistic pleasure, the market transactions that give rise to profits are likely to generate some social benefit in the meantime.

Christopher Badcock in Chapter 3 suggests that the market both requires and facilitates cooperation. This is not just cooperation in the narrow sense of the minimal cooperation necessary to agree contracts. Rather, people understand that certain values and modes of behaviour are necessary to promote their own welfare and that of others in the positive sum game of the market economy – the most obvious value perhaps being trust. This is not true of a socialist economy where resource allocation is a zero-sum game, and where I may get less if my neighbour gets more. Badcock also has a lesson for politicians. If tax rates are too high, taxpayers will withdraw their cooperation, will practice avoidance and even evasion (or, in Arthur Seldon's phrase, 'avoision'), and yields will fall. Politicians need to know their limits!

Antony Flew in Chapter 4 asks why the 'profit motive' is

treated with such derision. We all respond to different price signals. One form of price signal is not necessarily any more or less noble than another. Workers and managers try to obtain higher wages; the owner of a holiday cottage tries to obtain higher rents; consumers want lower prices. But one never hears commentators use the phrases 'wage motive', 'rent motive' or 'price motive' with the same sense of derision as when they use the phrase 'profit motive'. Yet, in each case, we have individuals merely going about their business trying to pursue their own interests with a sense of purposefulness and without harming the interests of others.

A more benign climate of opinion for market ideas helps politicians to be braver both in their rhetoric and in their actions. Perhaps politicians have been too apologetic for the market economy – recognising it creates wealth but ignoring its other virtues, such as the way it induces cooperation, restrains bad behaviour, and so on. This might restrain us from exploring the proper domain of the market.

This monograph is a contribution to the debate on the relationship between morality, the market and virtue. It is of course not the end of that debate. It argues a strong case that the market economy restrains the powerful, engenders a spirit of cooperation and puts our baser motives to good social use.

If you really want to experience a vicious Hobbesian war of all against all, then look to a non-market economy where resources are fixed, where power and influence are all that matters, and where a contract cannot be trusted. What a contrast with the openness, the scope for personal fulfilment, and the sheer diversity of a modern market economy.

DAVID WILLETTS

January 2004

As in all IEA publications, the views expressed in this book are those of the authors and not those of the Institute (which has no corporate view), its managing trustees, Academic Advisory Council members or senior staff.

The front cover

Front cover image of farmers (sic) market in Seattle, WA, by Terry Healey. Image of church by Adam Kowaltzke. Composite image created by Brill Design.

ACKNOWLEDGEMENTS

One of the contributors to this collection, Professor David Marsland, was particularly interested in the overall character and arguments of the book and offered many helpful suggestions. I am most grateful to him. My thanks go also to my wife, Mary, as always my closest and best critic. Finally, I would like to thank anonymous referees for their helpful comments.

DENNIS O'KEEFFE

SUMMARY

- Commentators often praise markets for their wealth-creating abilities but doubt the capacity of a market economy to promote virtue. Because of this, many intellectuals tolerate rather than welcome market economies.
- The same commentators often suggest that markets are characterised by selfishness. However, the self-interest that is, in fact, an important characteristic of individuals acting in a market economy is not the same as selfishness. To regard self-interest as the same as selfishness is an objective error.
- The market economy restrains the harm that selfishness can do to others. The protection of property rights, together with the requirement for contracting parties to consent to market transactions, means that the potential of evil people to do harm is limited in a market economy.
- In an economy that is centrally planned, those who are motivated by selfishness will not gain from mutually beneficial transactions, but rather they will gain from working their way up to a point in the political system at which they become entitled to material goods as perquisites.
- The fact that individuals respond to profit opportunities tells us nothing about their moral outlook. To have more information about an individual's moral outlook, one would have to know how the individual used the profits from market transactions.

- The obvious manifestation of a market economy, as seen by the critic, is 'getting and spending'. However, we cannot know a person's motives or the extent to which they are concerned for others by simply observing the process of 'getting and spending'. To conclude that the market economy is characterised by materialism because we observe 'getting and spending' is like concluding that the earth is flat because that is all we see directly with our eyes.

- The market economy both requires and facilitates cooperation. This is not just cooperation in the narrow sense of the minimum cooperation necessary to agree and enforce contracts but, more widely, cooperation that promotes certain values and modes of behaviour that are necessary for people to promote their own welfare and that of others in the positive-sum game of a market economy.

- Commentators sneer at and treat with disdain the 'profit motive'. Yet other maximisers within the market economy do not suffer such treatment. Commentators do not complain about a 'wage motive' or a 'price motive' when people try to take the best advantage of market situations in other contexts. Yet, in general, all those involved in market transactions are trying to pursue, purposefully, their interests, without harming the interests of others.

- Free choice to pursue a course of action and alternative courses of action is essential if decisions are to be regarded as 'moral'. Morality is therefore not possible without freedom.

- Socialism encourages anti-social behaviour through the design of its welfare systems. It treats the means of production, including human beings themselves, as chattels of the ruling class or of the state, to be used for the benefit of a 'greater good'.

Economy and Virtue

1   INTRODUCTION
Dennis O'Keeffe

What is the connection between the indispensable production of wealth on the one hand and the equally vital moral life of society on the other? What, to employ the words of our title, are the links between 'economy' and 'virtue'? The present collection of essays is primarily devoted to examining the part that markets have played and must continue to play in the moral life of societies whose economies are based on free enterprise, that is on private property and the relatively free play of supply and demand. Inevitably there is also in these articles some discussion of the kind of moral life generated by socialist economic systems, that is societies where property is socialised and the state 'plans' the composition of output. There is also by obvious extension some discussion of what might be termed 'sectoral' or 'residual' socialism, the kind characterising certain parts or pockets of predominantly capitalist societies. This latter combination of market and state production was at one time known as the 'mixed' economy.

Sectoral socialism has some institutional features in common with general (society-wide) socialism, namely a heavy reliance on public finance and sometimes on public property and central planning. Of equal significance to our concerns is that the moral life of the public sector in market economies has a good deal in common with the moral life of socialism proper. There are the same problems of widespread moral hazard and dedicated rent-seeking, problems that have come to be typically associated with remote and irresponsible elites.

Even in the post-communist era, the notion that market-based economic life is typically superior morally to state-based production is still very far from established. The governing view among intellectuals, at least in social science and the humanities, remains that private wealth is more productive of moral ill than moral good. This is the ancient theme that 'money is the root of all evil', the age-old legend of filthy lucre. The notion that the ownership and pursuit of wealth lead to moral corruption has still not died. Indeed, the present combination of attitudes is a very odd one. As Israel Kirzner points out in Chapter 4, the moral critique of capitalism has strangely survived the general realisation of its functional necessity.

The principal focus of the collection is on the positive links between markets and moral goodness. In most of the papers the critique of socialism, positive and moral, is nevertheless at least strongly implicit in arguments explicating the moral as well as the technical superiority of the market order. Certainly the starting point of all the authors is the moral desirability of the open society and the imperative that free men and women should organise their own lives to the maximum extent possible. This view necessarily takes cognisance of the disastrous results that flow from the critique of private property, profits, the money economy and the whole apparatus of the market, once that critique becomes a programme.

In Chapter 2 Walter Williams asserts that the first principle of freedom is that each person owns himself. This idea of sacrosanct property is the basis on which crimes against the person are forbidden. Capitalism depends on individuals having a sense of themselves. In this much more than markets is involved. Preservation of formal and informal institutions and moral agreement is necessary to a free society since it is clear that freedom is not a natural or inevitable part of the social world. Professor Williams is particularly anxious to dismiss false justifications of economic success and failure. Freedom and affluence (or their lack) are not to be mechanistically explained by resource endowment or population size, nor by colonial background. The moral superiority of free market systems, because they are based on voluntary exchange, is even more important than their manifest technical superiority. Governments sometimes reduce the economic welfare of their citizens by reckless policies and sometimes excessively cautious restrictions. We find examples of both errors when it comes to what drugs citizens may use. Sometimes governments curtail the general economic welfare by pandering to interest groups, for example in the imposition of measures to restrict competition from abroad. Williams takes an uncompromising stand on letting citizens work out their own preferences wherever possible.

In Chapter 3, Dr Christopher Badcock finds an instrumental morality at the heart of all social life. He shows that much social existence is characterised by a spontaneous search for cooperation. Cooperation is the spontaneous logic of the market. Markets rely on a morality intrinsic to them, rather than on external moral or political control. The fundamental moral choice within markets is between paying your dues like most people or cheating in some way so that others end up paying for you. There is in society a minority of free riders, and another minority tending to altruism. From the tension between these poles arises a majoritarian practice of rational compromise, in which people undertake not to defect from agreed norms. Across a wide range of human affairs, Badcock shows that self-interest can lead to social cooperation based on non-defection. When the search is for compromise, even a violent response may be predicated not on revenge but on restoring or maintaining cooperation. Parties with opposed interests learn that they gain mutually more by co-operation than either side would by defection. This is of great significance in the case of taxation. If governments cooperate by not setting taxes too high, citizens will cooperate by contributing more tax revenue. The proof that the inherent logic of social life is not always a zero-sum game is shown by the phenomenon of reduced tax rates by government, followed by *increased* tax revenue.

The socialist moral and positive critique of capitalism has, however, always been vitiated by a one-sided economic psychology, a psychology that concentrates arbitrarily on the alleged evils of profits. Profits are, in socialist mythology, the greed-driven dynamic of capitalism. This is the burden of the Marxist critique of the free market and its apparatus, by far the most influential one to date. It is true that neo-Marxism, as opposed to the classical credo, has undone some of the assumptions of rational self-advantage attributed to the capitalist class, by attributing to that class racial and sexual prejudice. Such prejudice cannot be exercised without denting profits. If women or non-whites represent a more economic use of labour than men, any capitalist refusing to employ them is thereby sacrificing profit maximisation.

The more convincing case, however, *à la* Milton Friedman or Thomas Sowell, is that modern capitalism is functionally indifferent to questions of colour, sex, and so on. Furthermore, there is deep confusion in the anti-free-market camp as to profit-seeking and its role in production. In Chapter 4, Professor Antony Flew disputes the old idea that production driven by the search for profits is intrinsically immoral. When *soi-disant* socialism goes morally astray this is taken as a deviation; in the case of market economies it is seen as characteristic. Flew stresses the arbitrary way in which a pyschological term, the profit motive, is imported into economic discussion without being accompanied, in a logical extension, by the *wages* or *salary* motive. If we are to take one economic category – profit – for use in an economic psychology, on what grounds do we not also have wages motives, salaries motives and the rest? It is also wrong to assert that interested parties are always selfish. The hostility to commercial economy is an ancient tradition going back to Aristotle, and represented in the nineteenth century by writers like Ruskin, and in our times by writers like Raymond Plant. In fact it is in the nature of commerce that it is *not* one-sided. When socialist experts decide what people 'need', as in the former Soviet-type economies, they deliver goods and services of very low quality. The public-choice tradition in economics also shows that likewise the public sector in free societies is not driven by a real interest in people's needs.

In Chapter 5 Israel Kirzner affirms that the view that to secure high living standards we have to tolerate an economic system that motivates people through greed, dishonesty and ruthlessness is indeed widespread. Indeed, though the free market has become an increasingly popular idea, this popularity has not been accompanied by any decline in the view that markets work through their appeal to immorality. This carries the danger that any experience of economic difficulty could result in a resurgence of anti-capitalism. In reality the coordinative properties of markets would be no different if market participants pursued saintly motives. Where economic decisions are taken by saints, firms will still try to get the highest price and pay the lowest wage. The price system depends not on selfishness but on the ubiquity of human purposefulness. Profits are only instrumental goals; ultimate goals or purposes can be either materialist self-devotion or altruism. In practice entrepreneurs may in any case build care for their workers directly into their operational calculus. Markets are morally neutral in so far as unethical behaviour is not required for the operation of the market system. Though humans are morally imperfect creatures, that imperfection is not the motor of market economies.

In Chapter 6 Professor David Marsland confronts the moral shortcomings of socialism. He sees socialism as deeply destructive morally, an inherently immoral form of governance, because both its larger-scale versions, such as communism and fascism, and its smaller versions, such as 'democratic socialism', with its accompanying welfare-state culture of dependency, destroy the market, along with other means and expressions of human individuality. Markets are constitutively virtuous as well as efficient. Totalitarianism, by dissolving liberty and choice, dissolves the differences between right and wrong; hence the banality of its outrages. Rule of law, limited government and economic prosperity are all integral to the development of virtue. Markets both challenge outmoded powers and preserve threatened liberties.

The Marxists claimed that markets are morally adverse and many less outlandish claims have identified them as neutral. In reality they are neither bad nor neutral, but on the contrary necessary both to the prudential virtues and to the whole panoply of values in the Judaeo-Christian tradition. Communism and fascism destroyed the market and thus destroyed the moral life of their peoples. So-called 'democratic socialism' in the form of the welfare state, with its accompanying dependency and aimlessness, rots the virtues more slowly and stealthily but nevertheless inexorably.

It is possible to argue that in plunging people into a common poverty, making most people poor, socialism was in a real, if adverse, sense more 'equalising' in its effects than is the market economy. On the other hand, socialism created wider gaps between the favoured elite and the impoverished mass than we ever find in an advanced market economy. Professor Shenfield says accordingly, in Chapter 7, that socialism produces a less equal society than capitalism, reviving differences in the goods and services available to different groups reminiscent of the old aristocratic/peasant distinctions of pre-industrial times. Shenfield says the market economy can cater for many different moralities, but that on the whole it is slanted in favour of virtue. Nor is the market economy either atomistic or destructive of solidarity. Nor are its virtues inferior to aristocratic and working-class virtues, admirable though these often are. Markets do, however, require impersonality and prudential morality. The failure of socialism is implicit in its trying to apply familial values to extensive production. Markets can serve many purposes, moral, immoral or neither; but the legal framework usually inclines them to virtue. There is little support for hostility to wealth in either the Old or New Testaments. Private property involves people in extensive moral training.

One of the most crucial aspects of political and economic arrangements is the impact of social assumptions. For competent economic arrangements it is necessary that the assumption that people can properly manage their lives be generally widespread. Social administration must assume individuals to be responsible and competent. Public welfare ('welfare' in its misappropriated sense of 'welfare state') encourages its beneficiaries to be neither. In Chapter 8, Dr Peter King echoes Charles Murray's American argument that social disaster has followed the discovery of so-called 'structural' poverty, in which the poor came to be regarded as helpless in the face of impassable barriers to their progress. British social policy too now assumes that structural poverty means the presence of individuals too weak to cope. There is also the presumption that no one should feel to blame for his own poverty or guilty about the public support he receives. Such policies have bad consequences morally and financially. People on welfare support adjust their aspirations to what such support makes available. Modern communitarianism seeks to break with the old socialism in re-establishing personal responsibility; but in its opposition to free markets it still ends up assigning too much power to the state. An individualist approach to social administration is called for, with the state neither pre-emptively judgemental nor willing readily to rescue individuals from the consequences of freely committed acts. Implicit in King's primarily sociological analysis is a recognition that, deprived of market discipline, people lose their moral independence.

In Chapter 9, Dr Sean Gabb argues that contrary to common impression the Internet will prove to be much more a promoter of moral good than of vice. In increasing exponentially the rapidity and scope of communication, the new technology hugely widens choice. Indeed, it goes some way to bringing together a reconciliation of neo-classical economic reasoning with that of the Austrian school, since it so improves the degree of perfectibility of knowledge in markets. The way in which improving markets widens choice is by definition a good thing, since morality is meaningless without the reality of choice. True goodness presupposes alternatives. The possibilities of unregulated and unknowable communications are becoming infinite. The privacy and swiftness of modern communication will in net terms make the citizen more rather than less secure than before. Political skulduggery by public figures will, however, be much less possible, as a relentless eye can be kept on their proceedings. Neither politicians nor media barons will be able to silence or intimidate us any more. The pressures on freedom of expression are breaking down. Though there are vile things on the Internet, this is a small price to pay for the huge increase in freedom it has created.

2 THE ARGUMENT FOR FREE MARKETS: MORALITY VERSUS EFFICIENCY[1]

Walter E. Williams

Introduction: freedom, sacrosanct persons and property

Friedrich Hayek said, '[f]reedom can be preserved only if it is treated as a supreme principle which must not be sacrificed for any particular advantage'.[2] Freedom's first principle is: *each person owns himself.* The preservation of capitalism – and by extension the transition from socialism – requires what philosopher David Kelley calls the entrepreneurial outlook on life, what he describes – in part-definition – as 'a sense of self-ownership, a conviction that one's life is one's own, not something for which one must answer to some higher power'.[3] If we accept as a first principle that *we each of us own ourselves*, what constitutes just and unjust conduct is readily discovered. Unjust conduct is simply any conduct that impedes an individual's property rights in himself when he himself has not first violated those of others.[4] Acts like murder, rape and theft, whether committed privately or collectively, are unjust

---

1   This chapter was originally published in the *Cato Journal*, 16, autumn 1996. It is reprinted here with permission from the Cato Institute.

2   Friedrich Hayek, 'Principles and Expediency', in Chaiki Nishiyama and Kurt R. Leube (eds), *The Essence of Hayek*, Hoover Institute Press, Stanford, CT, 1984, p. 301.

3   David Kelley, 'The Entrepreneurial Life', *IOS Journal*, 4(4), 1994.

4   We add the phrase 'when he himself has not first violated those of others' to allow for fines, imprisonment and execution when a person has infringed upon the property rights of others.

because they violate persons and private property. Persons and property must be seen as sacrosanct.

Widespread consensus that governments must not sponsor murder does not obtain vis-à-vis government-sponsored theft

While there is broad consensus that government-sponsored murder and rape are by definition unjust, however, far less consensus has been achieved regarding government-sponsored theft. Theft I define here as the forcible taking of the rightful property of one person for the benefit of others, a point to which we will return.

For individual freedom to be viable, it must be a part of the shared values of a society, and there must be an institutional framework to preserve it against encroachments by majoritarian or government will. Constitutions and laws alone cannot guarantee the survival of personal freedom, as is apparent where Western-type constitutions and laws have been exported to countries lacking traditions of individual freedom. In the USA the values of freedom are enunciated in our Declaration of Independence: 'We hold these truths to be self-evident, that all men are created equal, that they are endowed by the Creator with certain unalienable Rights, that among these are Life, Liberty and the pursuit of happiness.'

This value statement, serving such an important role in the rebellion against England and later the establishment of the Constitution of the USA, was an outgrowth of the libertarian ideas of thinkers like John Locke, Adam Smith, Sir William Blackstone and others.

Even in free societies like the USA the values of freedom have today been in some degree eroded

Even in societies with a tradition of the values of freedom, such as the USA, those values have suffered erosion and have proven an insufficient safeguard against encroachment by the state. Compelling historical evidence suggests, moreover, that personal freedom is not the normal state of affairs. We may only speculate why this should be the case. In any event, a general climate of personal freedom is not always self-reproducing, not always consistent, therefore, with stability. All too often political liberty is employed to seek monopolistic advantages. These result in the stifling of economic liberty, which in turn reduces political liberty.

It is basic values which bring economic efficiency and wealth, and not vice versa

Ultimately, the struggle to achieve and preserve freedom must take place in the habits and minds of men. And, as we are correctly admonished by the Constitution of the State of North Carolina: 'The frequent reference to fundamental principles is absolutely necessary to preserve the blessings of liberty.'[5] It is these fundamental principles that deliver economic efficiency and wealth, not the other way around. These fundamental moral principles or values are determined in the arena of civil society. Values such as thrift, hard work, honesty, trust and cooperative behaviour, based on shared norms, are the keys to improving the human condition, and they provide the undergirding for a broad market economy. Just as important, however, are social conventions, such as respect

---

5   North Carolina Constitution, Article I, Section 35.

for private property and the sanctity of contracts, and social institutions, such as schools and universities, clubs, charities, churches and families. These all provide the glue to hold society together in terms of common values and provide for the transmission of those values to successive generations.

Informal institutions are crucially important

All too often informal institutions and local networks are trivialised and greater favour is given to the narrow conceptions of intellectuals as to what constitutes knowledge and wisdom. In the event, the importance of informal networks formed by friends, church members, neighbours and families cannot be underestimated, as demonstrated in the following minor example of small proprietorships.[6] The critical determinants of a proprietor's success are: perseverance, character, ability, and other personal traits. Banks seldom finance the establishment of such businesses. Most small businesses are financed through sources like friends, family or the individual himself. In no small part, the reason is that these are the people who incur the lowest costs in acquiring the necessary information about those qualities deemed critical for a proprietor's success. Furthermore, friends and family who lend the proprietor money have a personal stake involved, that is an incentive to moderate their likely bias in favour of the borrower. Clearly, a formal lending institution could question friends and relatives. The information obtained would, however, have greater bias, since friends and relatives in this

---

6   The example is taken from Thomas Sowell, *Knowledge and Decisions*, Basic Books, New York, 1980, p. 25.

instance would have an insufficient personal stake to offset their personal bias in favour of the borrower.

Institutions and wealth

Hayek refers to what he calls rules of several property, determined by traditions and values: stability of possessions, transference of property by consent, and the keeping of promises.[7] Respecting private property and its transference *by consent* has produced a climate where mankind can more fully exploit the natural resources that surround him. This fact is almost too obvious to mention. Those nations having respect for rules of several property have produced a social and economic climate far more conducive to the welfare of their citizens than those having no such respect. That climate is one where voluntary exchange and free markets play an extensive role in the allocation of resources.

If we were to rank countries according to, first, whether they are more or less free market economies, second, their per capita income, and third, their ranking in Amnesty International's human rights protection index, we would find that those with a larger free market sector would tend also to be those with the higher per capita income and greater human rights protections. People in countries or territories with wide degrees of economic freedom, such as the USA, Canada, Australia, Hong Kong, Japan and Taiwan, are far richer and have greater human rights protections than people in countries with limited free markets, such as Russia, Albania, China and every country in Africa.

---

7   Friedrich Hayek, 'Origins and the Effects of Our Morals', in Nishiyama and Leube, op. cit., p. 321.

Natural resources and population size are not definitive in the development of wealth

People with a limited understanding of the role of private property and free markets claim that factors such as natural resource endowment, population size and previous conditions (e.g. a country might have been subject to colonialism) explain the presence or absence of wealth. In fact, by no means do questions of natural resources, population size and previous political conditions such as colonialism successfully explain a country's degree of human economic betterment. The USA and Canada are population-scarce and have a rich endowment of natural resources and *are* wealthy. If natural resources and population scarcity were adequate explanations of wealth, however, then one would expect nations such as the former Soviet Union and the relatively resource-rich/ population-scarce countries on the continents of Africa and South America to be wealthy. The sad economic experience of the former Soviet Union speaks for itself. And far from being wealthy, Africa and South America are home to the world's poorest and most miserable peoples. A history of colonialism is often given as an excuse for poverty, but that is a bogus hypothesis. The world's richest country, the USA, was formerly a colony. Canada, Australia and New Zealand were colonies and Hong Kong was still a colony until it was handed over to communist China. A far better explanation of the presence of wealth is the positive values and traditions that produce several property. Economic activity is not an independent variable whose laws are unaffected by the institutional framework within which it operates. Economic efficiency is a by-product of pre-existing cultural and moral norms.

The intellectual defence of liberty demands a moral rather than an economic argument

All too often defenders of free market capitalism base their defence on the demonstration that free markets are more efficient in terms of resource allocation and hence lead to a larger bundle of goods than socialism and other forms of statism. As Professor Milton Friedman frequently points out, however, economic efficiency and greater wealth should be promoted as simply a side benefit of free markets. *The intellectual defence of the free market should focus on its moral superiority.* In other words, even if the free market were not more efficient than other forms of human organisation, it is morally superior to these because it is rooted in voluntary relationships rather than force and coercion and respects the sanctity of the individual.

But the fact that free markets do produce a larger output themselves contributes to a more civilised society and civilised relationships. For most of mankind's existence, people have had to spend most of their lives simply eking out a living. In preindustrial society – and this still holds in many places today – the most optimistic possible outcome for the ordinary person was to be able to eke out enough to meet his physical needs for another day. With the rise of capitalism and its concomitant rise in human productivity, yielding seemingly ceaseless economic progress, it was no longer necessary for a man to spend his entire day simply providing for minimum physical needs. People were able to satisfy their physical needs with less and less time. This made it possible for people to have the time and resources to develop spiritually and culturally. In other words, the rise of capitalism has enabled the gradual extension of civilisation to greater and greater numbers of people. More of them today have time available to read and become educated in the liberal arts and gain more knowledge about the world around them. Greater wealth permits them to pay some attention to the arts; it affords them recreation, and the chance to contemplate more fulfilling and interesting life activities. They can now partake of culturally enriching activities that were formerly within the purview only of the rich.

Demystification of the state

A. V. Dicey wrote:

> The beneficial effect of State intervention, especially in the form of legislation, is direct, immediate, and so to speak visible, whilst its evil effects are gradual and indirect, and lie outside our sight … Hence the majority of mankind must almost of necessity look with undue favour upon government intervention. This natural bias can be counteracted only by the existence, in a given society … of a presumption or prejudice in favour of individual liberty, that is of *laissez-faire*.[8]

One can hardly determine the casualties of war simply by looking at survivors. We must ask what happened to those whom we do not see. Similarly, when evaluating interventionist public policy, we cannot evaluate it simply by looking at its beneficiaries. We must discover its victims. Most often the victims of public policy are invisible. To garner greater public support against government command and control we must somehow find a way to make those victims visible.

---

8   A. V. Dicey, 'Lectures on the Relation between Law and Public Opinion during the Nineteenth Century', London, 1914, p. 257. Cited by Hayek in 'Origins and the Effects of our Morals', in Nishiyama and Leube, op. cit., p. 316.

Victims of wrong policy, visible and invisible

In all interventionist policy there are those who are beneficiaries and those who are victims. In most cases the beneficiaries are highly visible and the victims are invisible. A good example is minimum wage laws. After the enactment of an increase in the legal minimum wage, politicians accompanied by television crews readily point to people who have benefited from the legislation. The beneficiaries are those with a fatter pay cheque. In this circumstance, the politician can lay claim to the wisdom of his legislation in increasing minimum wages. Moreover, the politician is himself also a beneficiary since those now earning higher wages will remember him when election time comes around. Furthermore, if the beneficiaries of the minimum wage are paraded across the stage, those who oppose minimum wage increases can be readily portrayed as having a callous, mean-spirited disregard for the interests of low-wage workers.

The political strategy of those who support liberty should be to expose the *invisible* victims of minimum wage laws. We need to show the facts about those who have lost their jobs, or have not been employed in the first place, because their productivity did not warrant their being taken on at the minimum wage. We should find a way to demonstrate that many jobs are destroyed by minimum wages. We must show how marginally profitable firms have been forced out of business, though surviving firms may have the same number of employees. We should show how capital was artificially substituted for labour as a result of higher mandated wages and how firms have adjusted their production techniques in order to economise on labour, such as in a greater use of plastic, throwaway utensils, fewer sections in entertainment arenas, fewer checkout stands, etc. The particular paths firms follow in order to adjust to higher mandated wages are less important than the brute fact that such adjustments will be made.

A more dramatic example of the invisible victims of interventionist state policy can be found in the regulation of medicines and medical devices, as in the case of the Food and Drug Administration (FDA) in the USA. Essentially FDA officials can make two types of error. They can err on the side of under-caution and approve a drug with dangerous unanticipated side effects. Or they can err on the side of over-caution, not approving a useful and safe drug, or creating costly and lengthy drug approval procedures.

Errors on the side of under-caution lead to embarrassment and possibly loss of bureaucratic careers and promotions because the victims will be made visible through news stories about sick people and through Congressional investigations and hearings. In the case of errors on the side of over-caution, through extensive delay in the approval of drugs, as in the cases of propranolol, Septra and others, the victims of the FDA are invisible, and their perpetrators go scot-free. Neither the victims nor their families know why they suffer or die.

Opponents of government interventionism must be made visible

These victims should be made visible. Once the FDA (or some other approving agency) approves a drug widely used elsewhere with no untoward effects, we should find people who died or needlessly suffered as a result of the FDA's delay. For political efficiency we cannot simply offer intellectual arguments. We must get pictures and stories of the FDA victims in an effort to appeal to a sense of fair play, decency and common sense among the citizenry.

But there is also a role for intellectual arguments in the sense of teaching people that any meaningful use of 'safe' must see safety as a set of trade-offs rather than a clear-cut category. The attempt to obtain a 'safe' drug means that people will die or needlessly suffer during the time it takes. That toll must be weighed against the number of people who might die or become ill because of the drug's earlier availability and attendant unanticipated harmful side effects. People should also be taught to understand that if a 100 per cent safe drug is ever achieved, it will be the *only* thing in this world that is 100 per cent safe.

A victim-finding political strategy can apply to other areas of state interventionism. One area that particularly applies to less developed nations is restrictive import laws and regulations. Restricting foreign imports as a means to save jobs sounds plausible. Adding to the appeal of restrictive trade policy is once again the fact that its beneficiaries are highly visible while its victims are invisible.

American trade restrictions as a case in point

Using an example of the American experience may suggest a political strategy. Most people fully understand that import restrictions raise the cost of products but may have little understanding of their systemic effects. Professor Arthur T. Denzau of the Center for the Study of American Business found that 'voluntary restraints' on imported steel saved nearly 17,000 jobs in the steel industry. The higher steel prices resulting from the restraints led, however, to a *loss* of 52,400 jobs in American steel-*using* industries. On balance steel restrictions led to a net loss of 35,400 jobs. The process is easy to understand. Caterpillar Company uses steel to produce heavy construction equipment. Trade restrictions cause higher steel prices which in turn raise its production costs. This makes Caterpillar Company less competitive in both domestic and international markets. That leads to downsizing of its labour force. As a result we see more Japanese- and Korean-produced heavy equipment in the USA. Importing finished products, though often not recognised as such, is just another way to import steel.

Trade restrictions destroy more jobs than they save and are costly to consumers

Trying to save jobs by way of trade restrictions not only destroys more jobs than it saves but is costly to consumers as well. According to estimates, the Reagan administration's 'voluntary import restraints' on Japanese cars increased the average price of Japanese cars imported to the USA by $900 and of American cars sold here by $350 for a total cost to consumers of $4.3 billion. That comes to a cost of $160,000 per year for each job saved in Detroit. Recognising this fact suggests that, from a national wealth point of view, we would have benefited immensely simply by striking a deal with Detroit auto workers whereby we gave the workers, who would have been laid off in conditions of free trade, $60,000 a year so they could buy a vacation residence in Miami. That way, collectively, we would have been better off to the tune of $100,000 per job saved. Of course, doing that would be politically impossible because the costs would have been apparent and Americans unwilling to pay it.

It is not only auto workers with whom the nation could have made such a deal. According to the Federal Trade Commission, 1985 quotas on textile products from Hong Kong cost consumers

$34,500 per year for each job saved for American textile workers earning $7,600 to $10,700 annually. Identifying the invisible victims of trade restrictions may suggest a political strategy to fight such restrictions. Those companies affected at second hand by trade restrictions could be organised to raise systematic protest. One such exemplary strategy would be to organise steel-using companies to make the damage done to them widely known, as in the case of the US steel import restrictions quoted above.

Justice concerns processes, not results

At the heart of most interventionist policy is a vision of justice. Most often this vision evaluates the presence of justice by looking at results. The idea of social justice has considerable appeal and as such is used as justification for interventionist statism. There are several criticisms of the concept of social justice that Professor Hayek has answered well, but defenders of personal liberty must make a greater effort to demystify the term and show that justice or fairness cannot be determined by examining results. The results people often turn to in order to determine the presence or absence of justice concern educational and occupational status, income, life expectancy and other socio-economic factors. But justice or fairness cannot be determined by results. It is a process question.

Consider, for example, three individuals playing a regular game of poker. The typical game outcome is: individual A wins 75 per cent of the time while individuals B and C win 15 per cent and 10 per cent of the time respectively. Knowledge of the game's *result* does not permit us to say anything unambiguous about whether there has been 'poker justice'. Individual A's disproportionate winnings are consistent with him being an astute player, a clever cheater or just plain lucky. The only way one can determine whether there has been poker justice is to examine the game's *process*. Process questions would include: Did the players play voluntarily? Were the poker rules neutral and unbiasedly applied? Was the game played without cheating? If the process was just – that is, if there are affirmative answers to those three questions – then there was poker justice irrespective of the outcome. Thus, justice is really a process issue.

In a free society income is earned through the provision of goods and services

The most popular justification for the interventionist state is that it creates or ensures fairness and justice in the distribution of income. Considerable confusion, obfuscation and demagoguery regarding the sources of income provide statists with copious quantities of ammunition to justify their redistributionist agenda. In reality income is not 'distributed'. In a free society, income is earned. People serving one another through the provision of goods and services generate income. People providing others with goods and services earn incomes, which in turn permits them to claim goods and services produced by their fellow men. The power of that claim is determined by the value their fellow men place on their production.

Money incomes are certificates of performance

We serve our fellow man in a myriad of ways. We bag his groceries, teach his children, entertain him, and heal his wounds. By doing so, we receive 'certificates of performance'. In the USA, we call these certificates dollars. Elsewhere they are called euros, yen or pounds. These certificates stand as evidence (proof) of our service. The more valuable our service to our fellow man (as he determines it), the greater the number of certificates of performance we receive and hence the greater our claim on the goods and services of others. This free market *process* promotes a moral discipline which says: Unless we are able and willing to serve our fellow man, we shall have no claim on what he produces. Contrast that moral discipline with the immorality of the welfare state. In effect the welfare state says: 'You do not have to serve your fellow man; through intimidation, threats and coercion, we will take what he produces and give it to you.'

The vision that sees income as being 'distributed' implies a different scenario, never made explicit, for the sources of income. The vision of income as distributed differs little from asserting that out there somewhere is a dealer of dollars. It naturally leads to the conclusion that if some people have fewer dollars than others the dollar dealer is unfair; he is a racist, sexist or a multinationalist. Therefore, justice and fairness require a redealing (income redistribution) of dollars. That way the ill-gotten gains of the few are returned to their rightful owners. This is the essence of the results-oriented vision of justice featured in most debates about public policy.

Those who criticise the existing 'distribution' of income as unfair and require government redistribution are really criticising the process whereby income is earned. Their bottom-line criticism is that millions upon millions of individual decision-makers did not do the right thing. Consider the wealth of multi-billionaire Bill Gates, the founder of Microsoft. Gates earned billions because millions of individual decision-makers *voluntarily* spent their money on what they wanted – his products. For one to say that his income is unfair is the same as disagreeing with the decisions of those millions of decision-makers. To make the argument that his income should be forcibly taken and given to others is to say that somehow third parties have a right to pre-empt voluntary decisions made by millions.

Low incomes tend to reflect low productivity

When sources of income are viewed more realistically, we reach the conclusion that low income, for the most part, is a result of people not having sufficient capacity to serve their fellow man well, rather than their being victims of an unfair process. *Low-income people simply do not have the skills to produce and do things their fellow man highly values.* Seldom do we find highly productive individuals who are poor, and the same applies to nations. People with low incomes tend to have low skills and education and hence low productive capacity. Our challenge is: how can we make these people (nations) more productive?

Governmental and other restrictions also help explain low incomes

Another explanation of low income is that the rules of the game have been rigged. That is, people do have an ability to provide goods and services valued by their fellow man but are restricted from doing so. Among these rules are minimum wage laws, occupational and business licensing laws and regulations and government-sponsored monopolies. Hence, we have one more argument for voluntary exchange and market allocation of resources – it is good for low-income, low-skilled people.

The vision of black markets

Finally, we should always keep in mind the resiliency of markets. Despite the efforts of socialist regimes, markets tend to survive to one degree or another. They are an irrepressible part of human nature. As Adam Smith said, 'It is the necessary, certain propensity in human nature ... to truck, barter, and exchange one thing for another.'[9] During the 70 years of the Soviet experiment, with massive attempts to suppress the market, including jail sentences, banishment and death penalties, markets in one form or another survived anyway. The conditions for the formation of markets are always present and explain their resiliency. Those conditions are: private ownership of property, interaction between people who place different valuations on goods, and individual will and self-interest.

These conditions give rise to markets, be they legal, illegal or black markets. According to some estimates, up to 84 per cent of the Soviet people purchased goods and services through the black market or *fartsovshiki*. The *fartsovshiki* was also a source of additional employment, and hence income, for as many as 20 million Soviet citizens. According to *Automotive News*, 60 per cent of Soviet citizens used black market mechanics for motor repairs and another 30 per cent purchased petrol and parts from black market distributors.

Soviet officials could never eliminate black markets and one doubts that they wanted to. After all, the Soviet system may have survived as long as it did because some of its uglier consequences were mitigated by the presence of black markets. Given the peri-

---

9   Adam Smith, *An Inquiry into the Nature and Causes of the Wealth of Nations*, ed. A. S. Skinner and W. B. Todd, Liberty Press, 1981.

odic shortages of life's necessities, such as food and clothing, there might have been uncontrollable social disorder if Soviet citizens had had to do without, rather than having a black market outlet to which they could turn for relief. Experience in the Soviet Union and elsewhere proves that man, left to his own devices, would be a capitalist. The transition from socialism to capitalism requires only that human nature be permitted to flourish.

Conclusion

Our struggle to extend and preserve free markets must have as its primary focus the moral argument. State interventionists stand naked before well-thought-out moral arguments for private ownership of property, voluntary exchange and the parity of markets. People readily understand our moral arguments on a private basis. For example, one person does not have the right to forcibly use another to serve his own purposes. People nevertheless see government doing precisely this as an acceptable use of coercion. If there is a democracy, that coercion is given an aura of legitimacy. The challenge for us is to present the argument that a majority consensus does not establish morality and that free markets are morally superior to other forms of human organisation.

3 THE MORALITY OF MARKETS: TAXATION AS A PRISONER'S DILEMMA

Christopher Badcock

Introduction

Cooperation and defection

Critics of free markets caricature them as 'anarchic' and motivated by 'greed' and 'selfishness', assuming them to be completely without morality unless regulated in some way, preferably by the critics themselves or the special interests for which they speak. But in its simplest and most fundamental form any uncoerced social relationship reveals very different characteristics. Let us begin with an example.

Suppose that you and an acquaintance go into a restaurant for a meal. Looking at it in the most basic terms, we might say that you and your partner could both obtain a benefit from such an event, and pay a cost. The benefit would be the meal, the cost the bill. But each of you would face a choice, either to pay or not to pay. Let us call paying the bill cooperating, and not paying it defecting. Now, there are four possibilities, depending on whether you cooperate or defect, and whether your partner cooperates or defects. If you both cooperate, you both pay and you both eat. We could call this reciprocity because cost and benefit are equally shared.

But now suppose that you cooperate and pay, but your partner does not, perhaps by claiming not to have enough money, or simply refusing to do so. We could call this altruism on your part in the sense that you paid for your partner's lunch. Looking at it from your point of view, however, we could claim that what your partner had done was to perform an act of selfishness because what he got out of it was a free lunch. Finally, we could imagine a situation in which neither of you was prepared to pay anything and so neither got any lunch. This we might call spite.

The Prisoner's Dilemma: individuals, groups and free riders

If we now think about the relative value of these outcomes to you or your partner, we can see that a free lunch is always best – you get a benefit without a cost. This is better than a lunch with a shared cost, because, in such a case, although you still get your lunch, you have to pay for it. But this is in turn better than no lunch at all, which, although it imposes no cost, also carries no benefit whatsoever. Finally, the worst outcome is having to pay for someone else's lunch – a cost without a benefit to you. Translating these examples back into the terms we defined in the previous paragraph, we can see that selfishness (a free lunch) is better than reciprocity (both eating, both paying), but that is in turn worth more than spite (neither pays, neither eats), and that the worst outcome is having to perform an act of altruism (you pay, the other eats at your expense).

For reasons to do with the anecdotes usually contrived to illustrate it, this set-up is usually called a Prisoner's Dilemma. A frequently voiced objection to it is that it can seem artificial and contrived. But the fact is that people often do face conflicts about cooperating with others to mutual benefit or defecting in their selfish interests, and it is important to recognise both sides of the basic dilemma, even if we would like to think that we would normally act in the social interest. The advantage of Prisoner's Dilemma is that it does present both sides, and balances them fairly, so that the outcome is not prejudged. Where markets and morals are at issue, Prisoner's Dilemma epitomises the simplest situation: two individuals in a market for cooperation based on free choice for each.

In general, group membership usually implies some cost to the individuals who constitute it, as well as some benefit. It is a fundamental principle of social science, however, that in a group of any size where this is true, individuals will always have a self-interest in obtaining the benefits of group membership without paying the initial costs or, alternatively, will have an interest in not paying an additional cost of membership from which they will obtain no more benefit than any other member.

There are always free riders, yet markets rely on morality

This problem is often termed the free-rider theorem, for obvious reasons. It sets out in terms of social theory what we all already know from bitter experience of the world: namely, that there will always be free riders who, at others' expense, try to gain the advantages for which they have never paid. Were this not a fact of life, public transport systems, markets and society in general would not have to be policed by various means, and sanctions would not have to exist to punish those who take without giving, benefit without contributing, or ride without paying. Markets rely on morality, and the fundamental moral choice is *that of paying your due like everyone else, or cheating in some way so that others end up paying for you.*

A case in point: car pooling for taking children to school

To give an example of how free riders can be dealt with, some years ago my wife made an agreement with another woman to cooperate in taking their children to school. The agreement was that one mother would take the children to school at the beginning of the day and that the other would collect them at the end. Obviously, both had a real incentive to cooperate in this way because it meant halving the time spent taking and collecting, petrol consumed, and so on. At first, all went well, but then, towards the end of the first term, the other lady's car began to let her down and my wife did significantly more journeys than she did. The holidays came and went, and the next term things got going on an equitable footing again. As the end of the term approached, however, the other lady's car once again began to be afflicted with mechanical problems. Finally, when exactly the same thing occurred at the end of the third term, my wife made a polite excuse and established another – and more successful – arrangement with another mother for the next school year.

Although a real-life situation, this was also a classic Prisoner's Dilemma, with an implicit set of pay-offs exactly comparable to the restaurant example. A free lunch or successful defection is represented by one mother having her children transported to school free of the very considerable charge represented by the time, petrol and general wear and tear on one's car and nerves involved. Being the sucker who pays for the other's free lunch represents the corresponding cost to the other mother of taking both her and the other's child to school each way. Mutual defection – spite – represents the cost to each woman of taking just her own child to school without any help from the other. Mutual cooperation means taking both children only half of the time, and is clearly less costly than taking both all the time or taking only one's own child both ways all the time. Both women were in a market for cooperation, and it relied on the morality of cooperation to exist.

Axelrod's computer games of iterated Prisoner's Dilemma

This real-life situation illustrates another dimension of Prisoner's Dilemma interactions: what happens when they are iterated, repeated over a period of time. Robert Axelrod[1] invited participants to submit computer programs to play iterated Prisoner's Dilemma. As we have already seen, Prisoner's Dilemma boils down to a simple choice of decisions, either to cooperate or to defect. The computer programs entered for Axelrod's tournaments each had to make such a choice with knowledge of the previous choices of its opponent (although obviously not of the current choice). Programs were played against each other in a round-robin tournament (meaning that each entry was played against every other entry), and scores totalled.

Two tournaments were played. In the first, fourteen entries were submitted by individuals with experience of Prisoner's Dilemma, coming from five disciplines: psychology, economics, political science, mathematics and sociology. Axelrod also entered *Random*, a program that made its choice to cooperate or defect a matter of chance and which came last in the first tournament and second to last in the second, indicating that some strategy was better than none. The winner was the shortest, simplest program submitted. Called *Tit for Tat*, its strategy was to cooperate on the

1   R. Axelrod, *The Evolution of Cooperation*, Basic Books, New York, 1984.

first move and thereafter do exactly what its opponent had done on the previous move. This was despite the fact that tit for tat was known beforehand to be a good strategy, and a number of the programs submitted were attempted improvements upon it. Analysis showed that neither the discipline of the author, the length of the programme nor its brevity could account for the result.

Tit for tat is not eye for eye: a World War I example

At this point it is important to correct a common misunderstanding relating to the question of the rule of reciprocity in establishing and maintaining cooperation. This is the view that the success of tit for tat represents a return to Old Testament-style eye-for-an-eye-and-tooth-for-a-tooth retaliation, the kind of thing that perpetuated the blood feud or vendetta and which, while it may sometimes encourage cooperation, also maintains violence, once started, in a self-perpetuating cycle.

A first observation might be that Old Testament-style retaliation begins with a defection rather than a cooperation, as tit for tat does. Blood feuds and vendettas always begin with the equivalent of a defection since they aim to avenge some wrong or to return some insult. A case which shows that reciprocity does not necessarily breed self-perpetuating cycles of violence is provided by one of the most dramatic real-life examples that one could wish to find of the role of tit-for-tat-style reciprocity in establishing cooperation. Historical accounts from World War I show that an astonishing live-and-let-live cooperation between the opposing armies emerged. A British officer who discovered it in a French sector recounted that it was maintained by means of the French firing only if fired on, but always returning two shots for every one fired at them. The fact that they retaliated with twice as much force as was directed at them shows that they were not following a crude eye-for-an-eye tactic, and the fact that it appeared to have established a surprising degree of peaceful cooperation suggests that it was not an example of a blood feud or vendetta mentality.

On the contrary, what the French were doing in this sector was what tit for tat did in the tournaments: not merely hitting back for the sake of some primitive law of talion, but reciprocating, not for its own sake, but in order to bring about continuing cooperation. This is why the French responded to the Germans with twice as much force as the Germans directed at them. But this is also why the French were never the first to shoot. What they were attempting to do was to induce peaceful cooperation in the enemy, by punishing them for their belligerent defections. Here reciprocity did not exist as an end in itself, but as a means to an end: cooperation with the other side, and, essentially, this was how tit for tat behaved in the tournaments. Its immediate and discriminating reciprocity was added to its other attribute: it was never the first to defect. Tit for tat in the tournaments was not the Prisoner's Dilemma equivalent of primitive talion, but a program which began by cooperating and which succeeded by encouraging its partners to cooperate, just as the French soldiers did with their two-for-one retaliations, but with a parallel reluctance to start any shooting.

The live-and-let-live system, whereby one side would inflict damage on the other only if the other inflicted prior damage, relied in large part on the fact that trench warfare produced a situation where small, evenly matched units faced one another for considerable periods of time. In other words, it was an iterated Prisoner's Dilemma, comparable to my wife's situation in the shared school run described earlier. As Axelrod points out in his discussion, cooperation in this situation was equivalent to avoiding damaging the enemy, while defection meant shooting to kill.

The self-interest of cooperating parties can motivate cooperation

The consequence of the behaviour was an astonishing and exquisite example of how cooperation can emerge spontaneously and be maintained, motivated purely by the self-interest of the cooperating parties. Like the triumph of tit for tat in Axelrod's computer tournaments, the emergence of the live-and-let-live system suggests that cooperation can emerge spontaneously, motivated solely by self-interest. Peaceable restraint, which originally began on both sides during mealtimes or bad weather, became extended to the point where open fraternisation became possible, and where on occasions soldiers on one side would actually apologise to the other for unintended breaks in the informal truce. Sniper or artillery fire, ostensibly intended to inflict damage on the other side, was in fact used as a means of maintaining the peace. Snipers would demonstrate their skill by repeatedly shooting at the same place on a wall to bore a neat hole, while artillery would show off their accuracy by hitting non-military targets. These apparently ritualised expressions of the conflict served to maintain the overall pattern of cooperation because they showed that, if necessary, the other side could be provoked into telling retaliation.

Such spontaneous order contradicts the view that order requires imposition or policing

This situation totally contradicts the widely held view that social order can emerge only if it is imposed or policed in some way – a question of morals rather than markets. The cooperating parties involved in the live-and-let-live system were not subject to any external authority enforcing the peace. They did not belong to the same society and did not share a common language or set of values. They had not been socialised to cooperate with their enemies, and their cultural backgrounds did not promote such fraternisation. On the contrary, the cooperating parties came from different cultural backgrounds which were at the time dominated by appalling nationalistic jingoism. Most outstanding of all, the fact that the participants in this astonishing display of international cooperation were subject to their respective High Commands and military disciplines, which were diametrically opposed to what they were doing, demonstrates that, even where external authority attempts to impose one kind of social order, order of a quite different kind can nevertheless emerge spontaneously, naturally and with greater effect.

This spontaneous moral order was destroyed by raids from outside the agreement

It is a sobering thought that the imposed social order so popular with moralists of all kinds was the very thing which worked against the live-and-let-live system, and which eventually destroyed it. The institution of unexpected raids, often carried out by troops not familiar with the local conventions, did much to undermine the implicit truces that had come to dominate long tracts of the front line. These sudden and vicious defections roused the enemy to retaliate in kind and undermined the trust and mutual confidence that had earlier built up so that eventually live and let live was replaced by kill or be killed.

Another aspect of the misunderstanding which sees the success of tit for tat as basically negative and retaliatory is found in the mistaken supposition that true reciprocity can occur only in the context of a zero-sum game. This is one in which anything gained by one side is a loss for the other (so that the sum of the minus points on the losing side and the plus points of the winner add up to zero). Most competitive games are like this, and so are all races in which competitors win or lose by their final placing. Just as the triumph of tit for tat demonstrated that cooperation can indeed emerge spontaneously in the market, so it also demonstrated that cooperation is not a zero-sum game, but that, on the contrary, both parties can gain more by mutual cooperation than either can gain by unilateral defection. An example almost as astonishingly counter-intuitive as the spontaneous live-and-let-live cooperation of World War I is provided by recent experience of tax reductions in both Britain and the USA.

The question of taxation resembles a Prisoner's Dilemma

On the face of it, nothing seems more obviously a zero-sum game than does taxation. After all, more for the government means less for the citizen and vice versa: the government revenue service's income is the taxpayer's loss. Yet, contrary to superficial appearances, taxation has some profound similarities to a Prisoner's Dilemma. To see why this is so, we have to realise that paying and collecting taxes do involve free choices and are a form of cooperation.

If the government sets tax rates at 100 per cent of citizens' income, taxpayers have absolutely no incentive to earn any income that could be taxed because they get nothing. If the tax rate is set at zero, however, the government gets nothing and the citizens retain all their income. Actual tax rates are always somewhere between these two extremes, so that in reality the incentive to earn or not to earn, and to pay or not to pay taxes, varies. In Prisoner's Dilemma terms, earning money on which taxes must be paid can be seen as the citizens cooperating with the government. Contrariwise, avoiding paying tax by not earning or by withholding or evading taxes can be seen as defection on the part of the taxpayer. Correspondingly, as far as government is concerned, reducing taxes can be seen as cooperating with the citizens, whereas increasing them can be seen as defecting.

Obviously, both taxpayer and government have an incentive to maximise their respective forms of income. Citizens would like to have all their income and pay no taxes, while government tax rates would reach their absolute maximum where all pay was taken as tax. Mutual cooperation implies both that citizens pay some taxes (and therefore have less than their total income to spend) and that government should take less than all the citizens' income in taxation. What both taxpayer and government get from mutual cooperation, however, will also be more than they would get if both parties defected by way of government imposing very high tax rates and citizens refusing to pay them. In other words, if taxation is a Prisoner's Dilemma, and if both parties defect as defined above, taxation could both be levied at a high proportion of citizens' income and be a small actual amount of money remitted to the government. This is because we have defined defection by the government as increased tax rates and because we have defined defection by taxpayers as reduced earnings on which taxes can be raised by the government.

At first sight, this seems impossible. How could high tax rates produce little actual tax revenue? The answer is contained in the earlier observation about marginal tax rates. At punitive marginal rates of taxation there is a strong incentive not to pay the tax, and plenty of perfectly legal means usually exist which allow the citizen not to do so – the most obvious being not to earn that particular form of income in the first place. Furthermore, recent experience certainly suggests that the pay-off to both government and citizens from marginal tax rates below an average of 50 per cent may indeed be greater than the pay-off to both at or above 50 per cent, at least for most groups of taxpayer.

The rich contribute more to tax revenue when taxes are low

For example, in Great Britain in the financial year 1978/9 the top rate of tax levied by the government was a punitive 83 per cent of 'earned' and a staggering 98 per cent of 'unearned' (investment) income. In that year the best-paid 10 per cent of the population contributed 34 per cent of all income tax collected. In 1989/90 the top rate of tax had fallen to 40 per cent but the top 10 per cent of earners now contributed 42 per cent of total income tax revenue in real terms.[2] Exactly the same effects are found if one concentrates on the top 5 per cent or 1 per cent of income earners. Not all taxpayers, it seems, are the passive victims of government policies, but they can respond actively in various ways, depending on the degree of cooperation with their income-raising activities shown by governments and their revenue-collecting services.

---

2   'Written answers to parliamentary questions', *Hansard*, 13 February 1990, col. 123, HMSO, London, 1990.

This is an important point in itself because critics of this approach to the analysis of cooperation often claim that real-life cooperative relationships are seldom comparable to the abstract, mathematical model represented by iterated Prisoner's Dilemma. For instance, some readers may well object to the foregoing discussion of taxation on the grounds that many taxpayers in reality have little choice because tax is deducted from their pay irrespective of their wishes and that their freedom to choose forms of incomes is very limited, if not completely absent in practice.

I will readily grant that this argument probably applies with special force at the extremes of income distribution. People with high incomes can and do have legal, financial and other opportunities which allow them to arrange their affairs to minimise their liability for tax – for example, by becoming tax exiles. Again, at the bottom of the scale, marginal rates of taxation may be sensitively reflected in workers' readiness to earn taxable income, as opposed to accepting untaxed payments in cash, not working at all, living on social security, and so on. Nevertheless, even people on middle incomes with apparently inescapable pay-as-you-earn tax liabilities show a surprising degree of resourcefulness in response to taxation. For instance, I know of a number of middle-income academics who could hardly consider another form of employment but who nevertheless have taken advantage of government grants for home improvement and tax concessions on mortgages to devote much time to buying, improving and then reselling houses. Because proceeds from the sale of one's own home are tax free in Great Britain, such incomes, although not realisable every year, can nevertheless be very considerable when they are earned. Indeed, one colleague openly admitted to me that he had costed out the income-generating effect of spending time building as opposed to writing to further his career and had found that, given the taxation regime applicable at the time, it paid him to build rather than to write! It seems that if governments can defect by raising taxes, citizens are not without means of defection of their own.

The surprising, counter-intuitive truths of mutual cooperation

I have found that some people react to the argument above – not to mention the fact that tax cuts have produced big increases in tax revenues while tax increases almost invariably realise less than expected – with something of the consternation with which the military and political authorities greeted the live-and-let-live co-operation in World War I. My guess is that what really scandalises them is the surprising, counter-intuitive truths that such examples reveal. These, as we have seen, are essentially three. First, that co-operation can and will emerge spontaneously motivated solely by self-interest and requires no necessary outside force, morality or innate altruism either to begin or to be maintained. Second, that social cooperation is not necessarily a more-for-one-means-less-for-another affair, but that, on the contrary, cooperation can and does produce more for all those cooperating than anyone could have realised by not cooperating. Finally, fundamental to both these effects is reciprocity – but not Old Testament, retaliatory reciprocity. Rather, this is reciprocity which exists not for its own sake so much as to make cooperation possible, to maintain it in a stable equilibrium, and to guarantee worthwhile pay-offs for all the cooperators.

Every social relationship is a Prisoner's Dilemma and mutual cooperation is the logic of the market

This, essentially, is the morality of the market. In the words of Adam Smith: 'It is not from the benevolence of the butcher, the brewer, or the baker that we expect our dinner, but from their regard for their own self-interest. We address ourselves, not to their humanity but to their self-love, and never talk to them of our own necessities but of their advantages.'[3]

Had we, in Smith's words, 'addressed ourselves to their humanity' we should quite clearly have been appealing to their morality. But Smith saw that markets were a superior alternative, commenting further that:

> man has almost constant occasion for the help of his brethren, and it is in vain for him to expect it from their benevolence only. He will be more likely to prevail if he can interest their self-love in his favour, and show them that it is for their own advantage to do for him what he requires of them. Whoever offers to another a bargain of any kind, proposes to do this. Give me that which I want, and you shall have this which you want, is the meaning of every such offer.[4]

In other words, every social relationship is a Prisoner's Dilemma if we reduce it to its fundamental terms: cooperate or defect. Mutual cooperation secures what both parties want, one-sided cooperation gratifies one at the expense of the other, and mutual defection punishes both by denying each the benefits of cooperation. The success of tit for tat depended on the fact that it

---

3   Adam Smith, *The Wealth of Nations*, Penguin, Harmondsworth, 1980, p. 119.
4   ibid., pp. 118, 119.

enshrined the simplest rule that will allow ongoing, stable cooperation to flourish: cooperate with cooperation, but defect against defection. Today we know that this is the fundamental principle behind cooperation throughout nature, from termite societies to human ones.[5] Markets, it seems, have a morality of which moralists proper know little or nothing.

5   C. R. Badcock, *Evolution and Individual Behaviour: An Introduction to Human Sociobiology*, Blackwell, Oxford, 1991.

4 SELFISHNESS, EXPLOITATION AND THE PROFIT MOTIVE

Antony Flew

Besides, there is nothing so plain boring as the constant repetition of assertions that are not true, and sometimes not even faintly sensible; if we can reduce this a bit, it will be all to the good.

J. L. AUSTIN[1]

There can be few more compelling examples of the sort of thing that the implacable Professor J. L. Austin hoped to reduce a bit than the constantly reiterated assertion that, because supposedly they are driven by the profit motive, competitive capitalist economies must be – as compared with the socialist command alternative – peculiarly and intrinsically selfish.

Immoral capitalism: from Tawney to Ramsay MacDonald to Einstein to Plant

Thus R. H. Tawney, to go no farther back, in his first prophetic book immediately after World War I, excoriated what forever after he was to view as a 'system in which industry is carried on, not as a profession serving the public, but for the advantage of shareholders'. He therefore wanted 'to release those who do constructive work ... to apply their energies to the true purpose of industry,

---

1   J. L. Austin, *Sense and Sensibilia*, Clarendon, Oxford, 1962, p. 50.

which is the provision of service'. He reflected with satisfaction, 'Over a considerable field of industry the Cooperative Movement has already substituted the motive of communal service for that of profit.'[2]

A few years later these thoughts were echoed by the then once and future Prime Minister Ramsay MacDonald: to transform 'capitalism into socialism ... industry must be converted from a sordid struggle for gain into a cooperative undertaking, carried on for the service of the community and amenable to its control'.[3] Much later still, a few months before his death, Albert Einstein was quoted in *Socialist International Review* as saying: 'The economic anarchy of capitalist society ... is the main cause of our evils. Production is carried on for profit, not for use.' And so it goes on, it seems, without end.

For in the summer of 1972, under the headline 'Waiting for a Sign from the Egoists', *The Times* of London reported that Archbishop Camara of Brazil had asked a meeting of members of both Houses of Parliament, 'Why do you not help to lay bare the serious distortions of socialism such as they exist in Russia and China? And why do you not denounce, once and for all, the intrinsic selfishness and callousness of capitalism?' Today Professor Raymond Plant – notwithstanding that he is often credited with having striven valiantly and with rare persistence to come to terms with the now no longer deniable failures of 'actually existing socialism' – still admits only grudgingly, 'There *may* well be a place for markets in a humane society' (emphasis added), while nevertheless strongly insisting that these must be

---

2   R. H. Tawney, *The Acquisitive Society*, G. Bell, 1921, pp. 140, 150, 152.

3   Quoted in S. H. Beer, *British Politics in the Collectivist Age*, Routledge, London, 1972, p. 136.

tightly confined, 'because they encourage some forms of behaviour rather than others, viz, egoism over altruism, and rational calculation of advantage over trust'.[4]

Why is it only profit which is psychologised?

To the archbishop's second question, the best first reply is another question: 'Why is it that we never hear of the rent motive or the wages motive?' Perhaps the classical distinction between profit and rent is obsolete. But if it is proper to speak of a profit motive, it should be equally proper to speak of a wages motive. By parity of reasoning we shall then have to admit into our new economic psychology the fixed-interest motive, the top-price motive, and the best-buy motive. Of course, if it is proper to argue that those who are paid wages must be stirred by the wages motive, then it has to be not merely proper but positively refined to say that those whose wages are paid at longer intervals and are called a salary or even compensation are inspired by, respectively, the salary motive and the compensation motive.[5]

The purpose of this immediate counter-question is to provoke two thoughts. First: that it is misguided to insist on applying to psychology a system of categories originally developed in, and ap-

---

4   K. Hoover and R. Plant, *Conservative Capitalism in Britain and the USA: A Critical Appraisal*, Routledge, London, 1989, p. 232.

5   The aptest comment for such prissy synonyms for the monosyllabic 'wages' and 'pay' is made by Bernard de Mandeville in *The Fable of the Bees*, ed. P. Harth, Penguin, Harmondsworth, 1970, p. 66:

> And when folks understood their cant
> They changed that for 'emolument';
> Unwilling to be short or plain,
> In anything concerning gain …

propriate to, economics. To insist on doing so is rather like postulating a set of chess motives, distinguished one from another by reference to those similarities and differences that have been found relevant to the interests and purposes of chess theoreticians, and then labelling these factitious postulations with expressions drawn from the technical vocabulary of chess – the knight's-move motive, the fool's-mate motive, the queening motive, or what have you.

It may perhaps be of interest to compare here a classic example of making a misguided move of this sort. For in *A Treatise of Human Nature*, David Hume contrived to discover that 'a man, who desires a thousand pounds, has in reality a thousand more desires, which uniting together seem to make only one passion; tho' the composition evidently betrays itself upon every alteration of the object, by the preference he gives to the larger number, if superior only by an unite.'[6] Noticing that suggestive 'thousand more', we may be tempted to go on to urge that before decimalisation the desire for a thousand pounds was – 'in reality' – 240,000 old penny desires, and that now it has been reduced to 100,000 new pence hankerings.

The second thought that should be provoked by that immediate counter-question is that, if you are going to introduce any member of some set of distinctively economic or distinctively chess concepts into your psychology, then it is altogether arbitrary to introduce one only without the others – to speak of the knight's-move motive without the queening motive, or of the profit motive without the wages motive.

6   David Hume, *A Treatise of Human Nature*, I, (iii) 12, Clarendon, Oxford, 1978, p. 141.

If it is not immoral to desire wages and salaries, why should it be so to want profits?

A second line of response to the challenge presented by Archbishop Camara is to insist that no one has any business simply to assume that the desire to make a (private) profit is always and necessarily selfish and discreditable, notwithstanding that the corresponding desires to obtain a wage or a salary or a retirement income are apparently not.

It is, no doubt, true that all these various desires are interested, in the sense that those who are guided by them are, in the immortal words of Damon Runyon, the Balzac of Broadway, 'doing the best they can'! But precisely because this does apply equally to all, we can find no ground here for condemning one and not the others.

This neglected fact is awkward for the denouncers. For no one, surely, is so starry eyed as to believe that any kind of economic organisation can dispense with all such interested motives. 'Every economic system devised for ordinary human beings,' we may read even in a tract otherwise devoutly socialist, 'must have self-interest as its driving force.'[7] If, therefore, one such system is upon this particular ground to be condemned as 'intrinsically selfish and heartless', then, by the same token, all must be. Yet that, of course, is not what is wanted by those who thus denounce capitalism root and branch while tolerantly discounting, as merely somewhat 'serious distortions', whatever faults they can bring themselves, however reluctantly, to recognise in socialism.

---

7   W. A. Lewis, *The Principles of Economic Planning*, Fabian Society, 1949, p. 7.

Interested actions are not necessarily selfish

There is a further and fundamental mistake here, and one that surely ought not to have been made by anyone with pretensions to act as a moral and spiritual guide. For, though selfish actions are perhaps always interested, only some interested actions are also selfish. To say that a piece of conduct was selfish is to say more than that it was interested. Selfishness is always and necessarily out of order. Interestedness is not, and scarcely could be.

For example, when two healthy children eagerly eat their dinners it would presumably be correct to say that each is pursuing his or her own interest; if any choices were involved, no doubt the economist would describe them as thereby maximising their utilities. Yet this is not sufficient reason to start reproaching them. The time for that is after the brother had grabbed his sister's dinner too, or perhaps in some less flagrant way refused duly to consider others and respect their proper claims. Even when my success can be won only at the price of someone else's failure, it would be inordinately austere to insist that it is always and necessarily selfish for me to pursue my own interests. Is anyone prepared to say that rival candidates competing for the same coveted position are culpably selfish in not withdrawing in order to clear the way for others?

The upshot, therefore, is that it will not wash to dismiss any one economic system as 'intrinsically selfish and heartless' simply because that system depends upon and engages interested motives, or even simply because it allows or encourages people to pursue their own interests in certain situations of zero-sum conflict. If there is something peculiarly obnoxious about wanting to make a (private) profit, it will have to be something intrinsic to (private) profit. It can hardly concern just wanting to acquire some economic good, or even competing to acquire scarce economic goods in any zero-sum conflict situation, as such.

Aristotle's critique of profit

That it is indeed essentially scandalous to make a profit and hence somewhat scandalous to wish to do so is an idea as old as the classical Greek philosophers. Consider what was said by the one who has had, and who, albeit mainly through Aquinas and Hegel, continues to have, by far the greatest influence.

Paradoxically the economic thought of Aristotle is found mainly in *The Politics*. One characteristic is that he accepts as normative whatever he believes to be, as it were, the intention of Nature. For those inclined to follow this lead, it should be salutary to discover where it took Aristotle:

> Now if Nature makes nothing purposeless or in vain, all animals must have been made by nature for the sake of men. It also follows that the art of war is in some sense a natural mode of acquisition. Hunting is a part of that art: and hunting ought to be practised, not only against wild animals, but also against those human beings who are intended by nature to be ruled by others and refuse to obey that intention. War of this kind is naturally just.[8]

No one after reading this will be surprised to find that the ideal universal provider envisioned by Aristotle is Nature, and not, as it

---

8   Aristotle, *Politics*, in R. McKean (ed.), *The Basic Works of Aristotle*, 1256B 20–26, Random House, New York, 1941, p. 1,137. It is perhaps worth emphasising that while some ancient Greeks argued that only barbarians (i.e. non-Greeks) ought to be enslaved, no one in those days ever suggested that this fate should be reserved solely for non-Caucasians.

would be today, the state. His position is thus oddly reminiscent of that of those contemporaries, both clerical and lay, who assume that all wealth, in the form of immediately marketable goods and services, was directly created by God and is therefore available, free of any legitimate prior proprietorial claims, for radical redistribution in accordance with the putative principles of 'so-called justice'.[9]

On a general view, as we have already noted, a supply of property should be ready to hand. It is the business of Nature to furnish subsistence for each being brought into the world: and this is shown by the fact that the offspring of animals always gets nourishment from the residuum of the matter that gives it its birth.[10]

It is significant that, after this high-minded classical formulation of the shabby familiar doctrine that the world owes us a living, Aristotle emphasises acquisition rather than production:

> The natural form, therefore, of the art of acquisition
> is always, and in all cases, acquisition from fruits and
> animals. That art ... has two forms: one which is connected
> with ... trade, and another which is connected with the
> management of the household. Of these two forms, the
> latter is necessary and laudable; the former is a method of
> exchange which is justly censored, because the gain in which
> it results is not naturally made, but is made at the expense of
> other men.[11]

---

9   It is, in Robert Nozick's happy phrase, 'manna from heaven'. Compare Antony Flew, 'God's Creation, Wealth Creation and the Idle Redistributors', in D. Anderson (ed.), *The Kindness that Kills: The Churches' Simplistic Response to Complex Social Issues*, SPCK, 1984; also Ronald Nash, *Poverty and Wealth: The Christian Debate over Capitalism*, Crossway, 1986.

10   Aristotle, *Politics*, 1258A 33–6, in McKean, op. cit., pp. 1,140–1.

11   ibid., 1258A 37–1258B 2, in McKean, op. cit., p. 1,141.

One point made here is that such exchange (trade) is in essence exploitation. Aristotle believes that the acquisitions of any trader must be made at the expense of that trader's trading partner, whereas the only creditable acquisitions are those achieved from non-human Nature directly. Shorn of these notions of what is and is not in accord with the intentions of Nature, Aristotle's is the same thesis, and the same misconception, as that which we find in *Unto This Last*: 'Whenever material gain follows exchange, for every plus there is a precisely equal minus.'[12]

This win-lose viewpoint has for centuries been, and still remains, a popular misconception, perhaps now especially in a form referring particularly to all trade in labour (power). For instance, an author who reveals no other Marxist cloven hoof states, as if it were the most uncontentious of truisms, that 'the mystique of capitalism … disguises the transfer of benefits from worker to employer under the form of an equal exchange of values, through the device of a free contract of employment'.[13]

Aristotle's seminal mistake here provides an always welcome occasion to quote a poet-scholar's rebuke to a rival scholar's lapse: 'Three minutes' thought would suffice to find this out; but thought is irksome and three minutes is a long time.'[14] The crux is that trade is a reciprocal relationship. If I am trading with you, it follows necessarily that you are trading with me. Trade is also, for both parties, necessarily voluntary. Nothing that you may succeed in seizing from me by force can, by that token, be either acquired

---

12 John Ruskin, *Unto This Last*, G. Allen, p.131. This fiercely anti-capitalist work greatly influenced both Mahatma Gandhi and most of the founding fathers of the British Labour Party.

13 David Miller, *Social Justice*, Clarendon, Oxford, 1976, p. 204.

14 A. E. Housman, *Juvenales Saturae*, rev. ed., Cambridge University Press, 1931, p. xi.

or relinquished in trade. If any possible advantage of trade to the traders could be gained only at the expense of some corresponding disadvantage to trading partners, it would appear that in any commercial exchange at least one party must be a fool, a masochist or a gambler.

Trade occurs because buyers want the goods and sellers want the revenue

But, as all must recognise when not either by theory or by passion distracted, the truth is that sellers sell because, in their actual situations, they would rather receive the price than retain the goods while buyers buy because, in their actual situations, they would rather pay the price than be without the goods. Ruskin was therefore wrong. It is of the essence of trade not that any advantage for one party can be achieved only at the expense of the other but that no deal is made at all unless both parties believe, whether rightly or wrongly, that they stand to gain thereby or unless at least both prefer the deal actually made to any available alternative deal and to no deal at all.

Certainly one of the trading partners, or even both, may be mistaken or in some other way misguided in the decision to deal. Certainly too the actual situation of either party, the situation in which it seems better to make the deal than not, may be in many ways unfair or unfortunate. But all this is contingent and hence irrelevant to the present question, which is: 'What is and is not essential to the very idea of trade?' Mutually satisfactory sex is a better model here than poker played for money. For in the former the satisfactions of each depend reciprocally upon those of the other, whereas the latter really is a zero-sum game in which your winnings precisely equal, because they are, my losses.

One temptation to conclude that trade necessarily involves a zero-sum confrontation lies in the fact that both buyer and seller would often, if they had to, pay more or accept less than they do. Obviously it is in such a situation possible to regard either the more that might have been gained or the less that might have been given as an advantage forfeited by one trading partner to the other. While this may often be the case, certainly it is not so always. Both buyer and seller may be, and I imagine typically are, simultaneously in similar situations with regard to such possible but unachieved advantages. It cannot be correct to infer, as a general conclusion, that all the gains of trade must always be achieved by one trading partner at the expense of the other.

Another less intellectual but in practice more powerful temptation lies in the unappealing human inclination rather to attend with eager jealousy to the gains of others than to find a modest contentment in one's own, to forget that the deal was to your advantage in order to resent that it was to his also. Surely he would not, as you so ungraciously insist, 'have made his profits out of you', had it not also been the case that you saw some advantage to yourself in your dealings with him? Yet how true it is that 'Few men can be persuaded that they get too much by those they sell to, how extraordinary soever their gains are; when at the same time there is hardly a profit so inconsiderable, but they'll grudge it to those they buy from.'[15]

---

15   Mandeville, op. cit., p. 113.

Aristotle's errors on usury: unless people cease to wish to purchase goods and services, abolishing money will not make them less mercenary

Aristotle's next contribution, equally unfortunate, has been equally important. The last passage quoted continues:

> The trade of the usurer is hated most, and with reason
> ... Currency came into existence merely as a means of
> exchange: usury tries to make it increase. This is the reason
> why interest is called by the word we commonly use [the
> word *tokos*, which in Greek also means offspring]; for as
> the offspring resembles its parent, so the interest bred by
> money is like the principal which breeds it, and it may
> be called 'currency the son of currency'. Hence we can
> understand why, of all modes of acquisition, usury is the
> most unnatural.[16]

'Usury' is now, thanks first to Aristotle and still more to his medieval successors, such a bad word that we may at first fail to realise to what he is objecting. It is not only to those very high rates of fixed interest that would nowadays be condemned as usurious. Nor even is it only to all fixed interest as such, which, as we shall soon see, was the prime target of those medieval successors. No, Aristotle's objection here is to any money return upon any money investment. It is, he thinks, against nature for money to breed money.

The moment Aristotle's point is appreciated, it becomes quite clear that both his objection and his supporting reason are superstitious and muddled. For a sum of money is the convertible equivalent of any goods or collections of goods that it might buy. There can, therefore, be nothing wrong in there being a return to

16   Aristotle, *Politics*, 1158B 2–8, in McKean, op. cit., p. 1,141.

money, unless it would be equally obnoxious and unnatural to ask for some return either in money or in kind for the use of the goods themselves.

Three corollaries may be drawn from this explication of the essential nature of money – corollaries the drawing of which makes these further references to Aristotle of more than merely antiquarian interest. First, it has to be entirely unilluminating psychologically to speak of any money motive and, by the same token, still more unilluminating to try to develop a complete economic psychology upon the basis of a series of economic distinctions between various mercenary motives. For that someone wants to make a profit or earn a wage tells us nothing of what he wants the money for. Almost any desire can take the form of a desire for money. It is obvious that this is a necessary consequence of the essential nature of money as a conventional instrument of exchange. Aristotle himself elsewhere makes this point about the nature of money. Nevertheless, as we have just seen, he fails to appreciate its present application.

The second corollary is that it has to be wrong to hope that the abolition of money, or even a reduction of the range of desired goods which money can buy, might by itself reduce greed and competition. Certainly it is tautologically true that the profit motive, the fixed-interest motive, the wages motive, and all the other factitious economic motives so far listed or suggested, are mercenary. All, that is, may be defined in terms of the acquisition of money. It might therefore seem that totally to abolish money or to reduce its importance as a means of acquisition must be to abolish or at least to weaken all mercenary motives.

In an appropriate empty sense, no doubt, this is true. Yet unless these changes happened to be accompanied by something quite different, an enormous transformation of present human nature, people would presumably continue to pursue, and to compete for, whatever it was that they had always wanted but that money could not now buy. In a word: if cars are not for sale for money but are available as a perquisite of public office, then this will by itself tend only to intensify the competition for such privileged official positions, a result long familiar to close observers of the Soviet-type economies (STEs) of eastern Europe. To abolish money would save us from being mercenary merely in the same empty way in which substitution of the word *gender* for the word *sex* saves us from sexist sin. For by itself, and short of the aforementioned total transformation of human nature, the abolition of money could not and would not so much as begin to make us either less materialistic or less competitive.

Money and trade greatly extend human choice

The third corollary is that money and the extension of the range of goods and services that money can buy are sovereign instruments of choice. If rewards are offered not in money but in kind, then recipients are precisely not allowed to choose: whoever fixes the rewards then determines not only their sizes but also what they are all to be. And if and to the extent that, for instance, health, education and welfare services are monopolistically provided by the state, then the citizens will be deprived of any direct and individual choice of what quantity and quality of such services they wish to consume.[17]

---

17 Compare, for instance, F. A. Hayek, *The Road to Serfdom*, rev. ed., Routledge and Kegan Paul and the University of Chicago Press, 1976, ch. 7; Ralph Harris and Arthur Seldon, *Overruled on Welfare*, Institute of Economic Affairs, 1989; and Arthur Seldon, *Charge*, Temple Smith, 1977.

In his *A Critique of the Gotha Programme*, Karl Marx proclaimed a distributive ideal that many have found appealing: 'From each according to their abilities, to each according to their needs.' Few, it seems, have caught the sinister overtones both of authoritarianism and of austerity in that slogan. (Perhaps these were missed even by Marx himself.) But necessities are most typically and naturally contrasted with luxurious superfluities; and although we are all of us the best experts about our own *wants*, it is others who are so eager to tell us that what we really *need* is altogether different, and usually disagreeable.[18] How too, save by compulsion, is it to be ensured, after all individual incentives have been eliminated, that all will labour at their prescribed tasks to the limits of their abilities?

The false and ancient notion that experts know the economic needs of others

Aristotle maintains, as quoted above, that trading exchanges are always essentially exploitative. In the same passage he makes a tricky and precarious distinction between the two forms of the art of acquisition: acquisition for household use and acquisition for financial gain. This surely must be the first forefather of an evergreen antithesis, that is, the antithesis between production for market exchange on the one hand, and production for the satisfaction of human needs on the other hand.

Though it is an evergreen, a moment's thought should show this antithesis to be false. Producers for a market cannot expect to make any profits at all save in so far as other people are able and

---

18 Compare, for instance, ch. 5, 'Wants or Needs: Choice or Command?', in my *The Politics of Procrustes*, Prometheus, 1981.

willing to purchase their products. Presumably those others – that is, we ourselves – propose in some way to use whatever we buy, judging that it is needed to satisfy some of our wants. What is most emphatically not guaranteed is that what ordinary people are able and willing to pay for will be improved on by the preferences of socialist intellectuals, preening themselves upon their egregious superiority to the unenlightened and vulgar, and ruling on that which we truly and properly need.[19]

The true antithesis here is, of course, that between a market and a command economy. In the former, producers produce what they believe they can find people able and willing to buy. In the latter, what is produced is whatever the actual power elite commands shall be produced, which is likely to be some combination of what they want for themselves along with what they decide is all that the rest of us really need. In the last few years, more information than ever before has become available about the preference structure of the actual power elite in the former USSR. What – to borrow General Lee's phrase for describing Union armies – 'those people' have most greedily wanted for themselves has been, in order to maintain and to extend their power, enormous and efficiently equipped military and police forces.[20] The residual output they have considered to be sufficient to meet the needs of the rest of the Soviet people is, by the standards of contemporary democratic capitalism, simply wretched.[21]

---

19 See, for instance, J. K. Galbraith, *The Affluent Society*, Houghton Mifflin, 1958.
20 Compare, for instance, Henry Rowen and Charles Wolf (eds), *The Impoverished SuperPower: Perestroika and the Soviet Military Burden,* Institute for Contemporary Studies, 1990.
21 See, for instance, Nick Eberstadt, *The Poverty of Communism*, Transaction Books, 1988.

The final, fatal flaw in the critique of market greed

There is a final, fatal flaw in the assertion that, because supposedly they are driven by the profit motive, competitive capitalist economies must, compared with the socialist alternative, be peculiarly and intrinsically selfish. The assertion depends on an invalid form of inference. This invalid form of inference proceeds from propositions about the purposes attributed to institutions and to the people establishing these institutions, to conclusions about the actual operative motives of the future managers and employees of these institutions.

There is no disputing that the management of any firm that wants to stay in business and has no access to any open-ended subsidy has to pay constant attention to the bottom line. Yet from this fundamental and undisputed fact about private business we are most emphatically not entitled to infer that to obtain and to maximise profits is necessarily and throughout all working hours the exclusive and overriding concern of that management, much less that which must be the predominant or indeed any very noticeable concern of all the employees.

To keep profitable is in the long run a necessary condition of staying in business. But that is by no means a sufficient or indeed any sort of good reason for insisting that the only motive that people can or do have for going into or staying in business is to obtain for themselves the maximum possible profit. Furthermore, not only is the argument leading to this cynical conclusion invalid but the conclusion itself is also in fact false. For very few of us ever manage to be so utterly single-minded about anything. Many, too, have had occasion to rue the fact that such a single-minded profit orientation was far from characteristic of some firms in which they themselves have invested. Everyone must, surely, have had plenty of experiences of friendly and considerate treatment that was quite obviously not motivated by a pure and exclusive pursuit of financial gain?

Nor, of course, is the fact that a particular productive enterprise is a state-owned monopoly, or that some other organisation was specifically established to serve the public interest, any guarantee that those employed in their operation will either already be or by these facts be encouraged to become not only more altruistic and less egotistic but also more trusting and less given to any 'rational calculation of advantage' than the rest of us.

If Professor Plant does sincerely believe that it is a guarantee, then it is very difficult to prescribe any likely effective remedy. Nevertheless, some introductory readings might help: technical readings in the economics of public choice[22] and/or some more agreeably entertaining readings of *Yes Minister*.[23]

The uncomfortable enquiry that should be pressed upon Professor Plant and upon all those others who share his intrusive interest in the motives of economic agents is simply: 'Why?' – or aggressively, 'By what right?' If people sell me satisfactory products at competitive prices, then it is surely no business of mine to pry into their motives for first acquiring these products and then selling them to me and to anyone else able and willing to pay the prices charged.

Such intimate investigations are properly left to their chosen spiritual advisers, if any. The most salutary example here for all of us is that of Queen Elizabeth I. She used to insist that she wanted

---

22   A good short starter is William C. Mitchell, *Government As It Is*, Institute of Economic Affairs, 1988.

23   Jonathan Lynn and Anthony Jay, *The Complete Yes Minister*, Harper and Row, 1988.

no windows into men's souls. It was enough for that most talented and liberally inclined ruler that her subjects, whatever their private motives and beliefs, should behave always as loyal and obedient subjects.

In general, and it is a reflection that has wide relevance, economic arrangements are best judged by results. Concentrate on the price and quality of the product. Do not officiously probe the producer's purity of heart. It is difficult to avoid diagnosing this eagerness to pursue such irrelevant and intrusive probings as springing from anything but a stubborn refusal to accept that socialism has most decisively failed the test of judgement by results, combined with a desperate hope that it might still be saved by an appeal to its supposedly altruistic intentions.

Where questions about motives are out of place, however, questions about interests may be very much to the point. For even the most minimally prudent persons must always hope, and try to ensure, that their suppliers have some interest in supplying them to their satisfaction; and this quite irrespective of whether or not these interests provide the main or sole operative motives of the suppliers. You do not need to be the total cynic to feel anxious about the quality and reliability of supply where the suppliers have no interest in giving satisfaction and where their clients have to depend on the universal presence and strength of 'the motive of communal service' – one of the goods that is notoriously almost always and everywhere scarce. The author of the first and greatest classic of development economics was, as usual, both humane and realistic when he wrote: 'It is not from the benevolence of the butcher, the brewer, or the baker that we expect our dinner, but from their regard for their own interest. We address ourselves, not to their humanity but to their self-love, and never talk to them of our own necessities but of their advantages. Nobody but a beggar chooses to depend chiefly upon the benevolence of his fellow citizens.'[24]

---

24 Adam Smith, *An Inquiry into the Nature and Causes of the Wealth of Nations*, ed. A. S. Skinner and W. B. Todd, Liberty Press, 1981.

5 ECONOMIC SCIENCE AND THE MORALITY OF CAPITALISM
Israel M. Kirzner

Introduction

In this paper we explore the old theme that economic science (more precisely, a flawed but widespread understanding of economic science) is at least partly responsible for the tragically mistaken view that a successful free market society must be an immoral society. That this view has enjoyed widespread currency will hardly be denied by anyone; and in some intellectual quarters it will not be doubted that this widespread currency was responsible in the twentieth century for disastrous public policies. The thesis under discussion here is that this mistaken view can be traced, at least partly, to an unfortunate understanding of economic science. A more careful understanding of the foundations of economics can make a contribution to a more accurate (and more favourable) moral image for capitalism.

The ethical misinterpretation of economic science

Throughout its history, economic science has explained the achievements of free markets in enhancing national wealth, in promoting socially gainful exchange and division of labour, in attaining efficiency in the social allocation of resources, in promoting economic coordination among members of society. Indeed, these teachings of standard economic science have led to its being recognised, by friend and foe of capitalism alike, as the intellectual foundation for any case for capitalism. Foes of capitalism have for over a century and a half recognised standard economic theory as the enemy which must be destroyed if capitalism is to be discredited in the market for ideas. Friends of capitalism have recognised the positive role of sound economics in generating understanding of and appreciation for the public benefits conferred by economic liberty.

Too often, however, economic science has been presented in a manner that sees these benefits as arising strictly from patterns of individual behaviour which most ethical observers denounce as immoral. The problem is, of course, an old one, and one well recognised. It goes back at least to Mandeville, who argued that 'what we call evil in this world … is the grand principle that makes us sociable creatures, the solid basis, the life and support of all trades and employments …' It led to early denunciations of economics by moralists such as Ruskin (who pronounced the classical economists, and those who could read their work with acceptance, as having entered into an 'entirely damned state of soul'). Economics seems to explain the success of a free market society by its reliance upon the untrammelled interplay of the decisions made by selfish, materialistic individuals. Economics has not, in public perception, been able to shake itself free from its dependency (in terms of arguing the efficiency and affluence of a market society) upon *Homo economicus*, defined in a way that portrays him, in Frank Knight's characterisation, as 'the selfish, ruthless object of moral condemnation'.

To be sure, modern economists of virtually all schools have, certainly since Robbins's 1932 *Nature and Significance of Economic*

Science, recognised that economic theory does not require selfish and materialistic agents, only agents who are 'rational', i.e. consistently self-interested (with altruistic motives being included as possible 'interests' of the individual). Yet the educated layperson might be excused for believing otherwise. Despite lip-service to the idea that the criterion for economic behaviour is no more restrictive than that it be concerned with optimal allocation of scarce resources for the attainment of objectives of all kinds, economists seem continually to be referring to a much narrower set of concerns. Despite Frank Knight's insistence some three-quarters of a century ago that the 'idea of a distinction between economic wants and other wants must be abandoned', economists (including some of his own most eminent disciples) continually measure economic success as if the notion of a specifically 'economic' objective for society is indeed well defined – as the maximisation of aggregate 'wealth' or 'value', measured in money.

People think we have to tolerate immorality in order to enjoy the advantages of capitalism

Consequently, close to three hundred years after Mandeville, public perception concerning the teachings of economics on capitalism is still mired in paradox. It is widely believed that capitalist prosperity derives from the freedom that the system offers to the greedy, the grasping and the gouging, to cheat and to exploit. Even if public opinion has, during the past decade, swung round towards a more favourable view concerning free markets, this has not meant that any more benign perception of capitalist morality has emerged. Rather what has happened is that a widely shared cynical attitude has crystallised, to the effect that the immorality of unbridled economic freedom is seen as a price worth paying for the enjoyment of the luxuries of Western capitalism. That such an attitude is a highly brittle one should be obvious: the enemies of the market have only to wait for any faltering in the growth of prosperity, for any reason whatever, in order to exploit the apparently obvious lesson. That lesson is that economic immorality does not, after all, pay. The paradox of Western economics, that economic immorality promises economic prosperity, will have been triumphantly exploded.

It is not true that the invisible hand depends on the acts of immoral people

If only for this reason alone, therefore, it is worthwhile to insist upon exorcising from economics those tendencies to see market achievements as the paradoxically benign outcomes of unethical behaviour. We must insist that it is one thing to claim that individuals acting strictly in regard to their own objectives are led, as if by an invisible hand, to coordinate their decisions with those being made by others. It is quite another thing (and quite fallacious) to insinuate that this invisible hand derives its cunning strictly from the moral failures of market participants. We must insist that the coordinative properties of free markets would be as fully relevant for societies of saintly altruistic market participants as for ruthlessly selfish and materialistic participants.

Hypothetical sainthood and the free market

It is perhaps worthwhile, in order to drive home this insight, to outline very briefly how a free market would operate in an imaginary society of saintly individuals in which each consumer is primarily concerned to help others, and engage in what we would ordinarily call consumption (such as eating, buying new clothing, and the like) only in order to be able to carry out his primary, philanthropic objectives. Sometimes it is thought, even by economists who should know better, that if everyone is selflessly concerned to help others, then the price system must collapse. Even if it is understood that utility maximisation by consumers can be held to apply even to such a selfless society (simply by recognising that a desire to help others must be incorporated into utility theory), yet it is thought that the price system must break down because of the absence of the profit motive. In a society of selfless saints there seems at first glance no way to incorporate a profit-maximising motive that might drive the price system in the way envisaged in microeconomic theory. Surely individuals for whom the well-being of others takes precedence over their own material consumption will not conduct their business affairs by charging their customers the highest prices they can obtain and paying their workers the lowest wages they can get away with. And if the compass of profit maximisation has, in such a society of saints, been abandoned, it would appear that the conclusions of price theory can no longer be supported. All the elegant marginal equalities demonstrated, as a result of the assumption of profit-maximising behaviour, in the theory of the firm must be given up. In this society of pure altruists none of the efficiency properties ascribed to a well-functioning price system would seem to hold. So might run the argument.

This argument is clearly quite mistaken. Identifying the fallacy that this argument expresses will be instructive in clarifying the nature and function of the business firm in the real world of capitalism-without-saints.

Capitalism-without-saints

The truth is that profit-maximising business firms, charging the highest possible prices, and paying the lowest possible wages, would emerge in the purely saintly society in exactly the same way as in ours. The profits won in business activity would, in the saintly world, no doubt be dedicated to lofty, saintly, philanthropic purposes, instead of being devoted to grossly selfish, materialistic enjoyments on the part of the successful entrepreneurs. But that is all. In conducting his business, an entrepreneur who has no interests other than to eliminate the ravages to humanity of dread diseases would act strictly on profit-maximising principles. By hypothesis his highest (in fact his only true) goal is to combat disease. All else (including enhancing the well-being of his workers, or of his business customers, not to speak of his own material well-being) must and will be subordinated to the overall objective of winning the greatest volume of profit in order to fight disease. The results demonstrated by the theory of the firm hold without modification.

The point is, of course, that to maximise profits is merely an instrumental goal. Saint and sinner alike may seek to maximise profits; they differ only in the uses to which attained profits will subsequently be dedicated. (In exactly the same way saint and sinner alike may drive on a highway from city A to city B, using the same road map and following the same driving principles; they differ only in the ways in which they will respectively enjoy city B's varied endowments.) The profit motive and thus the price system depend for their driving force not upon the ubiquity of selfish or materialistic goals, but upon the ubiquity of *human purposefulness*. In a society based on division of labour and freedom of entrepreneurial entry, those intent on attaining resources with which to fight disease, or other saintly objectives, have every incentive to engage in business ventures to maximise pecuniary profit.

Our purpose in emphasising this simple point is to throw light on the nature and role of the entrepreneurial firm in capitalist society. It is, after all, upon the objective of unadorned profit maximisation that most critics have poured their most mordant scorn. It is the profit-maximising entrepreneur who is seen as unfeeling, ruthless and selfish, as cunningly exploitative and chronically dishonest. It is because his activity is understood to be central to the workings of the free market that the market society is believed to rely upon systematically unethical behaviour for its driving force. But the truth is that profits are not ultimate objectives; only consumption objectives are. Profits are instrumental goals to be deployed for the attainment of immediate (consumption) objectives. The morality or immorality of pursuing profits depends entirely on the morality or immorality of pursuing those consumption objectives.

Moreover, it follows that the profit maximisation objective of business activity relies, as Philip Wicksteed pointed out 85 years ago, *not* upon selfishness but upon what he called 'non-altruism'. That is, to maximise profits implies not that the businessman is unable to recognise any higher purpose than his own enjoyments, but that he has some purposes that rank higher, at the moment, than the purpose of enhancing the welfare of those with whom he is now trading, to which he intends to dedicate the profits he wins. We might emphasise, perhaps in modification of Wicksteed's position, that we do not posit that purely profit-maximising entrepreneurs have no regard for the welfare of their workers and customers, merely that such regard ranks lower, on the entrepreneur's utility scale, than those other objectives for which profits are being pursued. It should be further observed that, while for theoretical purposes it is convenient to deal with the purely profit-maximising entrepreneur, economists have always been well aware that real-world entrepreneurs are free to modify the purely instrumental objective of maximising profit by introducing 'consumption' objectives (such as those of caring directly for the well-being of one's workers and one's customers) into one's 'business' activities. While the price system certainly does rest upon the concept of pure profit maximisation, the socially benign properties of the price system in the real world do not depend upon the existence in that world of only those analytically pure agents which people the theoretical system. There is no difficulty in applying price theory to a world in which businessmen integrate some of their consumption objectives directly into their profit-making activities; social coordination can be achieved through the free market also in a world in which businessmen do urgently and genuinely care for the well-being of their workers and customers.

In at least one sense capitalism is ethically neutral

It should hardly be necessary to expand on the obvious truth that to deny that capitalism depends for its success upon unethical behaviour is not at all to maintain that unethical behaviour is somehow excluded from or by the capitalist rules of the game. To point out that the economics of a free market society of saints need not be essentially different from the economics of real-world capitalism is not to anoint capitalists as saintly. The important truth surely is that, at least in one most significant sense, capitalism is an ethically neutral system, that is, it efficiently promotes the fulfilment of goals of all ethical stripes.

Certainly the capitalist economies encountered in modern economic history have not always been peopled by businessmen of overwhelmingly selfless, saintly or otherwise particularly ethical character. And there may indeed be sociological or psychological theories linking the morality of man's behaviour to the economic system (capitalist, socialist, or whatever) in which they participate (there is of course a considerable literature of conflicting theories in this regard). Our thesis is merely that the economics of capitalist prosperity – clearly the most arresting feature of the system – is independent of the particular ethical principles subscribed to by the participants in a capitalist society.

Property rights protect welfare even when entrepreneurs are morally corrupt

There is, however, one sense in which it may be important to relate capitalist success to an implication of capitalist rules of the game in regard to unethical individual behaviour. While capitalism is certainly consistent with grossly selfish or otherwise unethical behaviour, the property rights framework of capitalism is such as to eliminate the social harm one might be inclined to attribute to such repugnant behaviour. A consistently enforced and protected set of property rights must mean that however deplorable a person's behaviour may be, such behaviour is quite powerless to harm others in any literal sense. Without property rights, the selfish greed of one agent in the economy must rob the others of the potential use of the scarce social resources devoured by the greedy one. With property rights securely in place, greed may breed covetousness, it may be responsible for uncharitable behaviour; but in terms of any danger of this actually reducing the well-being of others, we must pronounce it to be quite harmless. Where the capitalist rules of the game are respected and upheld, A's unethical behaviour is simply unable to violate B's property rights. Not only, as emphasised earlier in this chapter, does the free market not depend upon unethical behaviour for its driving force, but in fact the free market system insulates its participants from any direct harm that might be perpetuated by unethical behaviour, however defined.

Why it is wrong to link free markets with greed: a summary

We are now in a position to sum up our reaction to the widely held cynical attitude that capitalist prosperity arises only because the free market encourages repugnantly selfish behaviour and the pursuit of contemptibly materialistic objectives. We may summarise our reaction in the form of the following assertions:

1   It is not the case that free market success in satisfying wants and coordinating purposeful plans, depends on any necessarily unethical (or even materialistic) set of consumption objectives being pursued by market participants.
2   It is not the case that such free market success depends on unethical behaviour by business entrepreneurs.
3   While the free market system is certainly (neutrally) consistent with all kinds of unethical behaviour by its participants, the rules of the system protect each participant from direct harm being perpetrated against him/her through the unethical behaviour of others.

Despite our apparent rejection of the central Mandeville thesis, that public benefits arise from private vices, we should not lose sight of a fundamental feature of the market system. This is that the wonderfully productive social arrangement based on division of labour, specialisation and entrepreneurial discovery and social coordination through the price system works by harnessing the productive powers of individual participants to further, mutually, the consumption purposes of other participants. This means that the standard of living a person enjoys in the market economy is also advanced by the participation in that economy of individuals acting unethically, immorally or repulsively (and that one's own participation furthers the purposes of those immoral and repulsive others). When we draw the seductive picture of 'economic harmony' in which everyone is 'helping' someone else and making himself useful to him, we insensibly allow the idea of 'help' to smuggle in with it ethical or sentimental associations that are strictly contraband. We forget that the help may be impartially extended to 'destructive and pernicious or to constructive and beneficent ends …' So that private vices may, certainly, generate public benefits. The moral neutrality that we have claimed for the market economy does not guarantee that the benefits which market participants derive from their participation may not have been indirectly generated by the ethically deplorable behaviour of others. Moral neutrality merely means that ethically deplorable behaviour is not necessary for the success of the market economy.

We can be serious in our concerns with ethics and morality and at the same time we may support and participate in the capitalist economy without compromising our ethical commitments. To do so will indeed not exempt us from the responsibility to condemn and reject the deplorable behaviour, the greed, corruption and deception that we continually encounter in free market (as in other) societies. But we may extend such support and justify such participation secure in the conviction that we are not thereby automatically endorsing such greed, corruption, degeneracy or deception. Greed, corruption, degeneracy and deception are not prerequisites for a functioning and prosperous market economy.

Economists can help discourage misunderstandings concerning the role of unethical behaviour in markets by distinguishing carefully between the form of the market economy in theory, and the substance that makes up the market economies of the real world. At the formal level there should be no scope for misunderstanding. At this level there is no need to measure a society's success in the misleading terms of aggregate material wealth, or income in purely money terms. At this level, the obtrusive reality of a world made up of the imperfect human beings we are need not delude us into concluding that the driving force for market coordination is fuelled by our moral imperfections.

With a clear understanding of the secret of capitalist success as consisting strictly of the human purposefulness of its participants (and the capacity of this purposefulness to stimulate entrepreneurial alertness leading to mutual discovery and coordination), we may, if we wish to do so as moralists, attempt to improve capitalist reality without jeopardising its blessings. We may pursue whatever courses of action that ethical (and didactic) wisdom can identify in order to uplift ourselves and our fellow human beings – without interfering with that delicate and marvellous spontaneous social process through which 'men who have never seen or heard of each other, and who scarcely realise each other's existence or desires even in imagination, nevertheless support each other at every turn, and enlarge the realisation each of the other's purposes'.

My plea is that economists should seek to present our science to the world in a manner which, precisely by emphasising the abstractions of pure theory, discourages that disastrously erroneous perception of the ethical implications of the free market process, which muddy thinking about complex reality all too frequently tends to project.

6 CHARACTER, LIBERTY AND SOCIAL STRUCTURE[1]

David Marsland

Introduction

Markets are virtuous as well as efficient

Even among protagonists of a free market society, there are some who claim that markets are 'morally neutral'. This allegation constitutes a dangerous concession to the enemies of freedom, and a foolish encouragement to their inclination to reduce markets to a subordinate, merely instrumental role in the structure of society.

In fact the judgement is comprehensively mistaken. Markets are not morally neutral. They both presuppose and generate virtue. Like any human institution they can, in the short term, be misused and abused. But in and of themselves they must be judged by any dispassionate observer to be morally beneficial and, like other naturally evolved spontaneous human institutions – such as the family, the local community and the nation state – constitutively moral.[2]

I argue in this essay that freedom and personal autonomy are pre-conditions of genuine morality, that they are optimised in market societies, and that market participation facilitates and stimulates virtuous actions. I then go on to examine the various

---

1   This chapter was previously published in *Society*, 38(2), January/February 2001.
2   F. A. Hayek, *The Constitution of Liberty*, Routledge, London, 1960.

enemies of the market and the damage that their arguments and action do to freedom and morality alike.

Markets are not mere instruments of economic efficiency, though certainly they are at least that, as even socialists now reluctantly admit. Markets are also key arenas for the expression and development of fundamental human virtues, and indispensable nurseries of moral action. We need a coherent philosophical and sociological analysis of the grounding of morality in freedom, and *ipso facto* in market institutions, if the plaintive socialist critique of capitalism is to be answered once and for all.

Freedom and personal autonomy are core conditions of full and genuine morality

Moral action presupposes choice. Virtue entails an opportunity for vice forgone. The gravest charge against totalitarianism is that its ruthless suppression of liberty dissolves the distinction between virtue and vice, and empties the concept of morality of any meaning. Hence the banality discovered in the perpetrators of the Holocaust and the barren amoralism of the Gulag regime.

Thus, morality is feasible only in conditions of liberty. Without personal autonomy, I can do neither good nor evil. Freedom is the logical, psychological and sociological pre-condition of virtue.

Apparent virtue displayed in conditions of unfreedom is mere habit, a product of unconsidered custom, or a lingering trace effect of some long-lost freedom. Morally correct behaviour, arising as a response to external sanctions rather than as a result of autonomous, rational choice, is properly to be classified as conformity – and its contrary as deviance, rather than as moral action, with *its* contrary in immorality.

Admittedly this analysis involves a substantial simplification of the complexities of the real world. Most social circumstances are characterised by a mixture of freedom and unfreedom. Even in free societies, conformity induced by external sanctions and the inculcation of good habits is an essential stage in the development of morality in children. Even, indeed, among the adult members of free societies, a few may be so degraded by habitual vice that the imposition of punitive sanctions may be necessary in order to restore their capacity for genuinely autonomous moral action.

Morality and virtue are to freedom and choice as oxygen is to breathing

In principle and in general, however, morality is linked to freedom and virtue to choice as breathing is associated with oxygen. Deprivation of liberty is a poisonous gas which fatally destroys the essential hallmark of humanity – our capacity to make rational moral decisions. Morality is constitutively rooted in freedom. Self-reliant autonomy is the indispensable source of creativity, excellence, concern for others, and virtue in general.[3]

Freedom, markets and morality

If liberty is the essential pre-condition of virtue, and if we are concerned to preserve or restore the rule of morality, we must study closely the social prerequisites of freedom. For unfree societies permit at best domesticated beasts behaving well out of mere

---

3   H. Arkes, *First Things: An Inquiry into the First Principles of Morality and Justice*, Princeton University Press, 1986; W. Roepke, *The Moral Foundations of Civil Society*, Louisiana State University Press, 1995.

habit and custom, and at worst a jungle of amoralism fit only to be ruled by the Lenins, Hitlers, Stalins and Mao Zedongs of modern socialism.

Analysis of the social structure of freedom is a more challenging and a more complex task than I can address comprehensively here. The history of the development of freedom covers many thousands of years of subtle evolution, involving many distinct peoples and civilisations, from biblical Israel through ancient Greece and Rome, Renaissance Italy, the Low Countries, Britain in many eras, and the USA. The social functioning of freedom is conditioned by many, various and mysterious structural factors whose operations have not so far been better than fitfully illuminated, even by the powerful intellects of such as Aristotle, Hobbes, Locke, Kant, Montesquieu, Burke, Smith, Spencer, Acton and Hayek.

The rule of law and limited government are crucial to moral development

The development of individualism as a concept and as a practice, represented archetypically in Antigone's resistance to Creon, is essential. A framework of law such as Israel, Greece and Rome in combination have bequeathed to us is necessary. Toynbee is surely correct in his claim that a sufficiency of external challenge is necessary if a people are to fracture the cake of custom and develop the scope for innovation which freedom requires.[4] But so too is an adequate level of economic prosperity and institutional strength sufficient to resist external pressures and defend incipient liberty against its internal and external enemies. Not least essential is a

---

4   A. Toynbee, *A Study of History*, Oxford University Press, 1989.

constitutional state that facilitates the gradual evolution of democracy while confidently inhibiting pseudo-democratic tendencies such as those represented by Jacobins and Leninists.

The list of structural pre-conditions of liberty should no doubt be extended beyond this short list of mine substantially. But however long we make it, it has to include, and in a position of high priority, the market. Certainly in the optimal case of the genuinely and securely free society, the market is absolutely essential. And even at the earliest stages of the development of freedom, and in societies where liberty is much more partial and fragile than we trust we can take for granted in modern Britain, the role of markets – as instruments of innovative challenge to outmoded authority and as mechanisms of protection for threatened liberties – is crucial.

Without the market, freedom and virtue are fugitive or merely pale anticipations

The free market is an essential component of the social structure of liberty, and *ipso facto*, given my argument above about the relations between morality and freedom, an indispensable component of the social structure of virtue. Thus, other than in free market societies, genuine freedom is infeasible except occasionally, partially and accidentally. By the same token, bona fide moral action and authentic virtue are impossible in societies lacking free markets except at best as pale, anticipatory shadows of themselves.

Markets are thus neither morally negative, as their most incoherently severe critics (from Marx through Lenin to Hitler and Stalin) have alleged, nor even, as more moderate enemies of the market (from J. S. Mill through the Lloyd George Liberals to the

British Labour Party and modern Social Democrats worldwide) persistently claim, morally neutral. They are, on the contrary, in several distinct senses, resoundingly and constitutively positive in their moral implications and effects.

Markets rehearse the psychological and social skills that underlie the Judaeo-Christian repertoire of virtues

First, markets are one of the several indispensable social pre-conditions of liberty, and as such prerequisite to any genuinely moral action. In the medium term, if not in the short term, *no market, no freedom, no virtue.* QED.

Second, in the nature of their modus operandi, markets require quite stringent moral underpinnings – the concept and practice of honesty, for example, to ensure fair dealing, and the virtues of thrift, diligence and curiosity as guarantors of the self-reliant enterprise without which, as Russia's current parlous condition sadly demonstrates, markets are infeasible.

Third, over and above and separately from their prerequisite requirement of moral behaviour, markets are also among the most important arenas for the display, practice and learning of moral behaviour. It is in the marketplace rather than in the private confines of the family or the parochial domesticity of the local community (let alone the superficial milieu of high society and the media) that real reputations are made on the basis of genuine images of authentically virtuous action. It is in the continually challenging, competitive environment of a market society, unprotected by family, ascribed status or political privileges, that we can best rehearse the psychological and social skills that underlie the virtues of diligence, discretion, honesty, fortitude, and all the rest of the repertoire of Judaeo-Christian morality. It is in worlds of work shaped by tough market criteria that young men and women learn what it really means to behave well.[5]

Fourth and not least, it is the market which, much more reliably than any charter of human rights or the latest politically correct commitment to 'multi-culturalism' and 'gender equality', underwrites the genuine equality of all human beings. Capitalism cannot perpetrate holocausts or subject minorities to underclass serfdom or bind women to exclusive concern with '*Kirche, Küche, Kinder*'. These are political, and usually socialist, actions, to which the markets of capitalist society are in principle antagonistic – since in the market it is only money incomes, and effort that is exchanged for money incomes, which count. Every other human characteristic is strictly and completely irrelevant.

Thus it is the concept of the market and the practice of capitalist institutions which in the last resort provide the ultimate guarantee of democracy, of that equality to which democracy gives realistic, practical expression, and of the whole moral system of our civilisation out of which equality and democracy have sprung.[6]

Ultra-socialist enemies of virtue

Since the market is a pre-condition of freedom, and since freedom is a prerequisite of virtue, opponents of the market are enemies of virtue. If we wish to restore, preserve and enhance the sway of morality in decadent Britain, we must, therefore, vigorously resist the arguments, the media campaigning and the politics of those who

5   D. Anderson, *The Loss of Virtue: Moral Confusion and Social Disorder in Britain and America*, Social Affairs Unit, 1992.
6   T. Sowell, *Markets and Minorities*, Blackwell, Oxford, 1981.

denigrate the market. In defending the market, we are standing up for morality itself.

The enemies of the market are for the most part, unsurprisingly, socialists. In this section and the next I address two brands of socialist opposition to free markets. I consider first the damage done to morality by the hardline socialism of communists and fascists.

National and Bolshevik socialism are at one in their complete opposition to free markets and their undiluted commitment to subjecting markets to centralised political control by the state apparatus. Alleged differences between fascism and communism in this respect are inconsequential, as Orwell recognised correctly in *Nineteen Eighty-Four*.

However, since fascism has been crushed by force of arms and communism by economic implosion, why worry, the reader might ask, about either of these primitive ideologies now that we have reached the twenty-first century? The answer is simple. Fascism, like the Hydra, is forever revivified, however many of its ugly heads we cut off. We should expect it in Africa, in Asia, in South America, and even perhaps restored in Europe. Communism is an even worse case, since, although the media and social scientists may forget it, it is still alive and well in China, where duplicitous 'market socialism' is the equivalent of the Leninist NEP which facilitated Stalin's puritanical restoration of thoroughgoing communist terror. In Russia the forces of communism remain, despite welcome movement towards democracy and a market economy, strong and threatening. They loom like a shambling ideological zombie, dead yet hauntingly powerful in the hearts and minds of millions of ex-Soviets.

We must, then, still grapple with the ultra-socialist opposition to free markets of fascists and communists. In this endeavour, it is not enough to condemn fascism narrowly for its anti-Semitism or to dismiss communism simply because its utopian economic policies failed completely. Beyond and underlying these grave deficiencies, the fundamental error of national and Bolshevik socialism alike is their antagonism to the liberty inherent in the market.[7]

Everything else follows from that: their incapacity to distinguish right from wrong; their willingness to resort routinely to genocide as an instrument of normal policy; their easy inclination to aggressive war; and their incompetence in scientific and technological development.[8] Germany lost World War II and Russia the cold war primarily because the anti-capitalist ideology of their leadership and their elites destroyed the morality of their people. Robbed of virtue, these two great peoples were left incapable of the persistent, effortful, energetic action that the free world under Roosevelt, Truman, Churchill, Reagan and Thatcher were able to call on from the citizens of liberal market societies.

The lesson is straightforward. Destroy the market and you condemn the people to purposeless amoralism. Yield to ultra-socialism in any of its tempting varieties, and within decades your country will lie in ruins.

Pseudo-democratic socialist enemies of virtue

A more immediate and more realistic threat to liberty, and hence to virtue, is presented by the soft or pseudo-democratic

---

7   Hayek, *The Fatal Conceit*, University of Chicago Press, 1991; I. Shafarevich, *The Socialist Phenomenon*, Harper and Row, New York, 1990.

8   J. Marks, 'Uncovering the Terrible Crimes of Communism', *Right Now*, January/March 2000.

socialism into which fundamentalist socialism has conveniently transformed itself in much of the world. Its primary expression, which the market apparently or allegedly accepted in the industrial sphere (after decades of vitriolic condemnation), is support for the welfare state.

The ideology and apparatus of state welfare, with whatever benevolent intentions it may be established, inevitably stifle the responsible, adaptive behaviour that freedom requires of those who would claim its precious benefits. Its bureaucratic structures strangle the natural, spontaneously developing cooperative institutions on which freedom depends – the family, the market, the legal system and the local community foremost among them. Its tangled web of rules and obligations destroys the capacity of free men and women to choose freely for themselves and to pursue their individual interests rationally. Its illegitimate seizure of moral control abandons the people to purposeless drifting, subservient dependency and aimless incapacity to choose and act for themselves responsibly and freely.

Fundamentalist socialism has failed, and is apparently being replaced. The soft socialists' Welfare State has failed at least as badly. We need to replace it with institutions more appropriate to a free people. If we are to maintain our liberties and defend virtue, we should liberate welfare from the shackles of the state. Instead, we should provide for ourselves a system of welfare which, in turn, liberates from the cramping oppression of the state that capacity for responsible autonomy which is of the essence of moral action.

We should, therefore, turn the Welfare State over expeditiously and lock, stock and barrel to the free market and voluntary agencies. Given the very substantial reductions in taxation and considerable improvements in efficiency that privatisation would permit, most of the population – all except perhaps 10 or at most 15 per cent – would be much better served than they are under the established state monopoly system. They would, moreover, have restored to them (with the marketisation of welfare) the liberties, the scope for moral action and the exercise of virtue of which the nationalisation of welfare has for decades – with disastrous consequences for the moral condition of the British population – deprived them.

Nor should these moral advantages be forfeited by mistaken arrangements in the special assistance programme, which would certainly be needed for the unfortunate and feckless minority for whom moral and economic self-reliance is in the short term too challenging. Its fundamental mission would be to shift people out of state dependency and back into the normal self-provisioning system as rapidly as possible. This is essential if we are to reverse and prevent the major destructive effect of the Welfare State as currently organised – its moral and psychological impact on the character of free people.

For the most damaging effect of the Welfare State is its impact on the character, motivations and behaviour of individual men and women. They are subjected to its comprehensive expropriation of their capacity for free and independent action, for self-reliance, for enterprising initiative, and for moral autonomy. *By nationalising care and by expropriating personal responsibility, the Welfare State creates and reproduces dependency.*

This process affects every level of society and every sphere of social life. Welfare by right and on demand inevitably destroys what free and civilised societies have always defined as *the fundamental characteristic of human beings – the capacity to make rational moral choices as a basis for independent action.*

Collectivist welfare damages the economy, cripples the dynamism of enterprise culture, fails to help those who most need help, and worst of all positively harms those it is most meant to help – by creating out of temporary unfortunates among our fellow citizens an underclass of welfare dependants. Still worse, their dependency is transmitted from one generation to the next by the fractured families that inappropriate welfare encourages. This in turn multiplies, generating a permanent and expanding underclass of moral incompetents.

Reform of the Welfare State is imperative for the improvement of the moral life of citizens

If we are to halt and reverse this tide of decay, radical reform of welfare is essential. Unless we cut the Welfare State back down to size by contracting out the prosperous majority and by handling minority special needs more rationally, its destructively damaging effects will worsen still further as its expansionary growth continues at an accelerating rate.[9]

Thus even the soft socialism of supporters of state welfare consists essentially, like the fundamentalist socialism of fascists and communists, of a programme for restricting the operations of the free market. And the consequences are identical in both cases: economic efficiency is reduced substantially and the scope for virtue is rendered nugatory. Socialist antagonism to the market produces at one and the same time economic and moral bankruptcy.

---

9   D. Marsland, *Welfare or Welfare State,* Macmillan, Basingstoke, 1996.

Pseudo-moralistic campaigning against the market

Even if we can manage to keep the hands of ultra-socialists off industry, and persuade the soft left to acknowledge the necessity of reforming welfare, we shall still face resistance to the market and thus a restriction on the scope for virtuous action that genuine liberty, uninhibited by state interventions, would permit. This continuing opposition to the free market would come from campaigning liberal, conservative, Christian and other non-socialist paternalists and collectivists, actively led no doubt by socialists, who have transferred their activity as a result of the demise of more direct socialism on the larger scale.

Indeed, resistance to the pseudo-moralistic campaigning against the market organised by such people is already as important as the fight against socialism. In the media, in higher education and in the schools, in relation to the environment, the privatised industries, multi-culturalism, gender, gay liberation, Third World poverty, the arms trade, etc., active campaigns are afoot to impose still further bureaucratic state controls on the operations of the free market. Manned by a combination of ex-socialists and wilfully utopian idealists, these campaigns ground their arguments not in socialist ideology as such, but directly in moral rhetoric targeted at the market.[10]

They should be answered unapologetically without the slightest concession to their merely fashionable concerns. For on all these fronts the case for the market is overwhelmingly powerful, and the campaigners' moral arguments are incoherent and empty. They rest on *adolescent appeals to emotionalism* (the meat trade,

---

10   A. O'Hear , *Nonsense about Nature*, Social Affairs Unit, 1997; D. O'Keeffe, *Political Correctness and Public Finance*, Institute of Economic Affairs, 1999.

modern farming, road building), on *fraudulent or grossly oversimplified science* (Brent Spar, global warming, nuclear energy, smoking), on *muddled and heretical theology* ('ethical' investment, public service so called, profits and incentives), and on *bizarrely amateur philosophical analysis* (feminism, gay liberation, equality).

Across the whole range of these campaigning fronts, the cant is mistaken and the market is more efficient and more effective by a large margin than the bureaucratic systems that these pseudo-moralists prefer. Moreover, unlike the state-regulatory alternatives, which would close up moral debate, market solutions to all these problems would leave the public, the media and politicians free, as they should be in a free and open society, to debate the complex moral issues involved carefully and to make considered, pragmatic policy decisions appropriate to such challenging issues.

Socialism or virtue?

Even quite sensible people construe the pair 'morals and markets' as a contrast instead of a coupling. I recall my late father – a C2 proto-Thatcherite Yorkshireman of considerable native intelligence – insisting that while socialism obviously could not work, it was a valuable ideal. I never managed to dislodge this pseudo-Christian hang-up of his, or to persuade him that an ideology as unrealistic, morally incoherent and infantile as socialism was almost as unattractive as an ideal as in practice.[11]

Of course the market needs moral and legal regulation, but so

---

11   L. Schwartzchild, *The Red Prusssian: the Life and Legend of Karl Marx*, Pickwick, 1986; J. Bardach and K. Gleeson, *Man Is Wolf to Man: Surviving Stalin's Gulag*, Simon and Schuster, 1998.

too does every institutional sphere in a democratic society, especially the state itself. The lesson of history and of common sense is that keeping the state under effective control is exceedingly difficult: 'unfettered capitalism' is a socialist myth, while unfettered socialism is a reality whose murderous effects have been endured across the face of the earth.

The key to keeping the state under control is to keep its scope minimal, and in particular to prevent it intruding on the proper, expansive sphere of free market institutions. For the market is not only incomparably more efficient than the state in the production and distribution of goods and services of every sort, it is also – and this is why it is efficient – better attuned to the moral concerns of the mass of ordinary people, and allows them the scope, which the state can never provide, for deploying and displaying the whole range of human virtues.

Virtue is a function of freedom, of which the market is a key component. Socialists are in the business of restricting markets and thus of curtailing freedom. We must choose, therefore, between socialism and virtue, between the liberty and morality of capitalism and the slavish amoralism of state domination, between the programmed condition of mere ants and a life of freedom and personal responsibility as human beings.[12]

---

12   G. Himmelfarb, *The Demoralization of Society: from Victorian Virtues to Modern Values*, Knopf, New York, 1995.

7 BELOW THE ANGELS: MORALITY AND CAPITALISM

Arthur Shenfield

Introduction

Men who are less than angels

Among those who oppose the free economy, or who are uneasy about it, there are many who agree that it is more efficient than any other but believe that it lacks any, or any sufficient, moral foundation. They are right to maintain that the ability to produce an abundance of wealth is not enough. People will not live for long with a system for which this is the sole recommendation. They want to feel that their economy is a just one, or at the very least no more unjust than may be unavoidable in any society of men who are far below the angels. The champion of the free economy is therefore under a duty to show that it meets the requirements not only of efficiency but also of morality.

Four allegations against capitalism

It would be tiresome to set out all the allegations of immorality that have been made – and usually hurled – against the free economy or free enterprise system. Many are merely the product of ignorance or malevolence or both. It suffices to direct our attention to the following contentions. They are linked with, and overlap, each other and embody the substance of all the allegations that merit examination:

1   The capitalist system produces a society of gross inequality of wealth and income. It is good for the rich but bad for the poor.
2   The capitalist system is based on greed, selfishness or self-seeking activity. Hence the greedy and the selfish come to the top.
3   The capitalist system is based on atomistic individualism, subjecting people to the impersonal forces of the market. Hence it undermines personal relationships and social virtues and, in particular, the feelings of compassion and brotherhood that constitute the Good Society, turning an assembly of men into a true society.
4   The bourgeois virtues that are claimed for capitalism are inferior both to the aristocratic virtues of honour and *noblesse oblige* and to the working-class virtues of comradeship.

What these attacks are directed at is always styled 'capitalism', not because the descriptions 'free' or 'free market' or 'free enterprise' economy are inaccurate, though they may be alleged to be so, but because their flavour is too attractive for the taste of the critics of the system, whereas enough venom can be injected into the description 'capitalism' to give it a pejorative sound. The champion of the free economy does not need to reject the name 'capitalism', for it is quite acceptable. Nevertheless, it is not the most accurate name for the system of freedom.

Inequality

We need devote little time to the contention that capitalism is good for the rich but bad for the poor. The fundamental truth is that it is the greatest uplifting force for the poor that the human race has known in all the millennia of its existence. The very idea that the masses could ever be lifted out of poverty is a product of capitalism and its accompanying mentality. The masses are no longer poor. This means that the associated question of *inequality* of wealth and income merits greater attention.

There are three forms of equality which have attracted the minds of men: *equality before the law, equality of opportunity* and *equality of condition.* We may examine these in turn:

Equality before the law

Equality before the law distinguishes the free society. It is not the same as the rule of law, but closely associated with it. Such equality also goes with constitutional government. Without it justice between men is hard to envisage. This form of equality is also well capable of achievement. The shortfall from perfection arising from differences in access to the best, and therefore most scarce, forensic aid is insignificant compared with the shortfalls in almost all other social ideals.

Equality of opportunity

Equality of opportunity is elusive. Often it means simply the principle of *la carrière ouverte aux talents,* merely signifying that there are no legally upheld caste distinctions distinguishing one man's rights from another's. In this sense it is an unexceptionable corollary of equality before the law. Sometimes, however, equality of opportunity turns its face against *any inequalities* in access to schools, colleges, jobs, etc. It is one thing, for example, to say that no one shall be arbitrarily excluded from entry to the best universities. It is quite another to say that the inability of certain candidates to reach the intellectual standard required for entry to a top university in itself violates the principle of equal opportunity. When children from one kind of social stratum or one kind of school systematically fall below any achievement target compared with children from another, and this is regarded as violating 'equality of opportunity', the principle becomes quite inconsistent with equality before the law, requiring bolstering by arbitrary governmental action as well as by everybody being made equal at the starting gate of life's races. Here it calls for formal discrimination in favour of those allegedly suffering from some form of disability. Equality of opportunity in this sense is impossible – indeed, even proximity to it is impossible – and in practice its pursuit constitutes an excuse for the bestowal of governmental favour on easily identifiable groups supposedly suffering from past or present social inequities, whose pacification or electoral support is attractive to government. In other words the concept has illegitimately converged on – become almost indistinguishable from – that always undesirable goal, 'equality of condition'. To let students into college with lower grades than those of competing students, or into certain occupations with inferior results to those of other graduates because they come from poorer homes or less successful schools, offends against equality before the law.

Equality of condition

A policy for equality of condition calls for policies and practices inconsistent with the rule of law. It inevitably calls forth and relies upon envy and hatred. By its nature equality before the law must be in conflict with any scheme for equality of condition. Equality before the law is no respecter of personal differences, paying them no account and protecting the property of the rich equally with that of the poor. No man is greater than the law, and all are subject to it. It protects the sanctity of contract by whomsoever it is made. It defines torts and crimes by the *nature of the acts concerned*, not by the rank, identity or personal merits or demerits of the persons involved. Under such a principle, people's different endowments in intelligence, character, physique and the rest will produce inequalities of condition that will be protected by the law. The attempt at equality of condition requires that law be discarded in favour of the unremitting, arbitrary repression of those innumerable factors in life which produce inequality.

Equality of condition is a goal both impossible and immensely destructive

The goal of equality of condition inevitably summons up envy and hatred. Its pursuit is probably the most corrosive of all anti-social forces known to human society. Its most significant feature is its impossibility. Once the equality-mongers achieve power, it is quickly forgotten except as a slogan to divert the attention of the ordinary people from the privileges the rulers reserve for themselves. Consider Orwell's 'War is Peace', 'Freedom is Slavery', 'All Animals are Equal but Some Animals are more equal than Others'. If there are any innocent souls among the equality-mongers who meant what they said, they are soon disposed of.

A wide degree of a fairly equal condition is meritorious

In this sense it ill becomes socialists to assail the inequality of capitalism. Once achieved, socialism produces inequality more gross and obnoxious than anything observable in a developed capitalist country. Since there is some merit in a wide degree of a fairly equal condition in so far as it does not hinder desirable incentives or varieties of lifestyles, we should consider which kind of system is most likely to achieve it. The clear answer is capitalism. Socialism ostensibly pursues equality but in fact produces inequality. Capitalism pursues liberty but in the process reduces inequality. We have already noted that in capitalism wealth comes to those who serve the masses. Thus in capitalism the inequality of condition is little more than the difference between the Cadillac and the Chevrolet, the Parisian couturier's creation and the excellent mass-produced copies of it, caviar and the equally nutritious cod's roe. In pre-capitalist societies inequality of condition was the difference between the mansion and the hovel, between silk and rags, between exquisite luxury and frequent famine. In socialist societies it is that between the luxurious country villa and the miserable worker's flat, between the special shops carrying the high-quality goods imported from capitalist countries reserved for the party elite and the endless queuing for the shoddy products of socialist industry imposed on the masses.

Greed and selfishness are not externally distinguishable in market behaviour from altruism

Picture four men purchasing food in a market. Though their purchases are different, their behaviour is the same. Each seeks to obtain the best bargain he can. The first is a gourmand, the personification of greed and selfishness. The second is a gourmet. He too is concerned with self, but though we may criticise him on that score, we also admire his taste and we recognise that he may elevate the taste of others. The third is in the market to feed his family. There is a self-regarding element in this, but most of us will consider that his purpose is a highly worthy one, the hallmark of a man who discharges the most basic of his responsibilities. The fourth is the manager of an orphanage. His purpose is to feed the orphans and to do so to the best advantage permitted by the funds available to him. His purpose, we agree, is as unselfish as can be. Yet as we watch our four men in the market as they look for bargains and perhaps haggle with the vendors, we are unable to distinguish between them. The selfishness or unselfishness of their motives will be of no help to us. The orphanage manager may be the most determined bargain hunter and haggler of them all.

So, too, with men who seek to amass wealth. The aim of one may be to serve his grosser appetites, of another to serve his refined appetites, of another to provide ease for his family, and of another to endow a church, a university, a museum, or an orphanage.

This illustrates the naivety of the view that capitalism is based on greed and selfishness. Its business is to serve men's purposes, whatever they are; and its claim to our respect and admiration rests upon the indisputable fact that it serves them better than any other system known to man. It is for philosophers, priests and preachers to show men the way to the higher purposes. However elevated or debased their purposes may be, the market will serve them, save that, since the market itself requires a framework of law, the law will forbid the service of purposes that infringe the rights of other men and possibly also those that offend against some concept of public morality. For this reason the market is not neutral between elevated and debased purposes, but slanted in favour of the former.

It may be contended, however, that since most men have a large element of selfishness in them and some are wholly moved by it, the free economy, in serving their purposes, must be largely an engine for selfishness; and that, therefore, capitalism must be inferior to a system that controls men's purposes and positively directs them into the higher channels. This appears to be a plausible contention. But let us test it.

In fact capitalism and the care for the poor and unfortunate rose in tandem

First, for centuries in pre-capitalist times men were powerfully urged to practise the Christian virtues, to heal the sick, to succour the poor, to sustain the widow and the orphan, to avoid the seven deadly sins, in which forms of selfishness loomed large. Yet human life was cheap. Oppression was universal. Cruelty that would now appal us was commonplace. Punishments were inhuman. At the same time freedom to trade was limited and freedom of enterprise was repressed. It was no coincidence that the treatment of man by man became conspicuously more humane contemporaneously with the rise of capitalism. The ideology that produced the one also produced the other. But that was not all. The extreme poverty of the vast majority of people in pre-capitalist times made life cheap and invited inhuman treatment by the favoured few above them. It was the elevation of the standard of living of the masses which made such treatment progressively less possible. To take a not so trivial example, for centuries domestic servants could be physically chastised and made to sleep in holes and corners because no better alternative was open to them. The growth of capitalism can actually be traced by charting employers' complaints about the ever-rising demands of domestic servants for better conditions so that now only the very rich can afford them at all.

Second, consider the USA and Britain in the high noon of capitalism. These were the capitalist nations par excellence. If we are to credit the criticisms of capitalism, they should have displayed greed and selfishness to the nth degree. According to Carlyle and Ruskin, whose philosophy might be regarded as fascist, and the professors of Prussian socialism, they did. But suppose there was a famine, or an earthquake, or a volcano eruption in Timbuktu. Where first and most of all were subscriptions for relief funds opened? In the USA and Britain; not in statist France, or imperial Austria, Germany or Russia. Where were private charitable organisations of all kinds, covering all sorts of social and individual purposes, most typical and conspicuous? Again in America and Britain. The plain fact is that the environment produced by capitalism is of all those yet known the most conducive to the exercise of brotherhood and charity. All the critic sees is capitalist striving for getting and spending. In his view anyone with eyes in his head can see this and only this. So too, let it be remembered, can anyone with eyes in his head see that the earth is flat.

Atomistic individualism

Was there ever a doctrine more flyblown, despite its grip on many notable minds, than that which sees capitalism as the system of atomistic individualism, without the cement that makes a true society? Consider again the USA and Britain in the high noon of capitalism, and also Holland and Switzerland at a comparable time. Were there ever more cohesive societies than these, with people more imbued with a common pride in their society, the very special conflict of the American Civil War excepted? While the rest of Europe experienced revolution after revolution, the national unity of the British, the Dutch after the Belgians had detached themselves, and the Swiss, despite three main languages and diverse cantonal histories, wedded as they were to private property and to trade or industry, was unbroken by the political conflicts and controversies that they, like others, experienced.

The key distinction between state and society

The error here lurks in the failure of the critics to understand the distinction between the political and the social, between state and society. In his relation with the state, the free man insists on his individual rights. He requires government to be limited and circumscribed in power. He views the state not as a god but as one association among many, like his church, his club, his college, even his choral society or his pigeon fanciers' group, but he recognises it to be an association of very special importance, as he possibly also recognises the church. The critic sees this and accuses him of atomistic individualism. In treating the state as a mere association, it is said, he cheapens the bonds that tie him to it, and he deprives the state of the mystique that properly adheres to it.

The truth is otherwise. The free citizen takes a pride in his state precisely because its limited power obliges it to respect his freedom. His loyalty to it is thereby enhanced, not diminished. He does accord it a mystique, the mystique that enthuses him when he proudly declares that he lives in a free country. He knows very well that it is more important than any other association, except perhaps his church, which is why it is usually the only association for which he is ready to lay down his life. At the same time, precisely because the state respects his individual rights, he finds it natural and easy to enter into a web of voluntary relationships with his fellow men, which is the true social cement of his society. Contrary to the assertion of his critics, he knows very well that a society is more than a mere assembly of individuals, and he and his fellow men are much more successful in building it than are the members of any unfree society.

It is regrettable that many conservatives, who genuinely prize freedom but are made uneasy by individualism, do not understand this, and are therefore led to injure the capitalist system in the supposed interest of national unity or social cohesion. Thus they are ready to give tariff protection or subsidies to ailing industries in the presumed interest of the relief of distress or of social harmony, or under the illusion that they are actually strengthening the capitalist system. Given time, the result is always to shatter the cement of society, not to keep it whole.

The impersonal forces of the market in the Great Society

That capitalism subjects people to the impersonal forces of the market is true. This is an inevitable condition of existence in 'the Great Society'. This society gives each man enormous advantages.

Instead of being limited for his sustenance to whatever his family and close neighbours can provide, he is able to tap the resources of almost the whole world. At the same time the value of his service to others is greatly enhanced by the worldwide spread of the links between him and them. As Adam Smith told us long ago, the scope for the division of labour is the foundation of any civilised standard of living and indeed of civilisation itself.

Capitalism does not banish family values but an economy cannot be run successfully on familial values

Subjection to the impersonal forces of the market may at first sight be regarded as simply the price to be paid for great economic advantages. But are there only economic advantages? In the first place the Great Society does not exclude the personal relationships that govern a family or a small isolated community where all are known to each other. The members can continue to support each other with affection and respect in addition to material sustenance. In so doing they are aided immensely by the opportunities presented by their society, which requires them only to be ready to adjust to the ever-changing signals of the wants and offers of others. In the second place the personal relationships, benevolent or otherwise, of a family or small community cannot be transferred to a large society, for they depend upon everyone knowing everyone else. To attempt to run a large society like a family would produce either despotism or chaos. Indeed, the reason why socialism inevitably brings despotism or chaos, or a combination of both, is that it seeks to run a large society as if it were a family. Thus the emergence of the large society schools men in the nature and meaning of politics, thereby raising the stature of men. The market, which is the economic framework of the large society, thus brings more than mere economic benefit.

Bourgeois, aristocratic and working-class virtues

It has been a long time since the bourgeois virtues were the leading lights of our society. Work, saving, enterprise, sobriety, self-discipline, respect for the law, and the sanctity of contract – these no longer command the admiration that they did. But that may be the very measure of our society's decay. It is true that the aristocratic virtues of honour and *noblesse oblige* have great attraction, and it is arguable that the finest societies of modern times have been those in which the bourgeois and aristocrat meshed with each other, each learning something from the other's virtues, for example in Victorian Britain and the America once led by the New England–Virginia combination. But this is no reason to denigrate the bourgeois virtues. Even standing alone they clearly produce a more humane and elevated society than the aristocratic virtues ever did when they stood alone. Compare, for example, bourgeois Holland in the seventeenth century with aristocratic France. As for the working-class virtues of comradeship and perhaps patience, they are sometimes, but by no means always, admirable, but their leading characteristic is limited vision. To compare them with the bourgeois virtues is simply ludicrous. A society imbued solely with the working-class virtues could hardly rise above a primitive level.

The positive case for the morality of the free economy: property and moral training

So far we have considered the alleged immoralities or moral deficiencies of the free economy, and our concern has been to refute the indictment. We must now turn to the positive case for the morality of the system. We shall consider private property as an agent for moral training, the work ethic and the practical application of the principle of love for one's neighbour.

The private ownership of property is a central pillar of the free economy. The enemies of the free society correctly see that if they are to succeed they must direct their attacks against private property, perhaps in all its forms but at least in the form of the ownership of the means of production. In fact private property is an indispensable agent for training in morality, and therefore its central position in the free economy makes for morality in the system. But first we must consider the legitimacy of private property itself.

Neither moral philosophy nor religion cast serious doubts upon private property

It is difficult to find anything of consequence in the propositions of moral philosophy or the teachings of religion or the prescriptions of great lawgivers to cast doubt on the legitimacy of private property. Of course, there are many denunciations of the misuse of property, or of the pursuit of wealth above more worthy purposes, but in the wisdom of the ages the ownership of property is per se legitimate and even praiseworthy. The well-known observations in the New Testament which suggest that men would do well to dispose of their property and completely abandon the accumulation of any wealth at all have very rarely, if ever, been treated as a prescription for the generality of mankind or for a world not about to enter a messianic age.

In any case, they are hardly consistent with the general tenor of the Gospels, which assume the existence and maintenance of private property, and they are entirely inconsistent with the lessons of the Old Testament, including those features of it which the Gospels do not seek to amend or improve upon. Witness the vineyard owner in St Matthew who asks, 'Is it not lawful for me to do what I will with mine own?' and is in no way rebuked. Witness righteous Abraham, the Lord's chosen, who is blessed with great wealth. Witness upright Job, who, when he comes triumphantly through the terrible tests that Satan is allowed to impose upon him, is rewarded by the Lord not merely with the restitution of his ample property but by the doubling of it. Clearly private property was legitimate in the eyes of the Lord. Witness the good husbandman who constantly receives the praise due to a worthy character. In general, the ownership of private property has no need to excuse itself.

Defending the private ownership of the means of production

But what about the ownership of the means of production? In Marxist theory this is the great determinant of the character of society and its historical development, and in the capitalist era the source of all evil.

Non-Marxist socialists have also directed their attacks against the private ownership of the means of production. Is there a case for the view that this category of private property may be illegitimate? The owner of the means of production is a capitalist. His ownership, it is said, enables him to dominate the lives of others, especially the workers. Such a power, it is alleged, should not exist.

These contentions do not even begin to survive analysis. First, the alternative to private ownership is common ownership. Does common ownership of the means of production not dominate the lives of men? Only if one assumes that the decision-makers in common ownership think only of the interests of the people and also know what those interests are and how to serve them. This is a nonsensical assumption. 'Common ownership' is not really *common* ownership, but private ownership of a specially harmful character. The rulers of the 'commonly owned' means of production are thereby invested with power over the people to the nth degree, and they use it. But even if they wish to use it in a wholly benevolent way, they cannot know how to do so. They do not have the signalling system necessary for such a purpose. By contrast the private ownership of the means of production in the capitalist system is dispersed and thus in competitive hands. The idea that it dominates the lives of the workers is really a variant of the false notion that the worker is at an inevitable bargaining disadvantage with the employer.

In any case, what is meant by the means of production? They are always assumed to be the factories, plants and machinery; in short, what the capitalist owns. But we have already noted that labour is necessary to give these means of production their value. The truth is that labour is itself a means of production. So, too, are all the other inputs in the production process. In fact, almost anything can be a means of production.

Private property and virtue

We have established the legitimacy of private property. We can now pass to its positive virtue. Picture the good husbandman. As with devoted care he raises the fertility of his fields and improves the quality of his livestock, always concerned to pass on his trust in finer shape than that in which it came to him, we watch him and admire him. This, we feel, is how a man should live. Whatever God or Nature, according to belief, puts into his hands he should use with diligent care, treat as a trust, and pass on to his successor in a condition to be proud of. The same admiration ought to be aroused by the good factory, mine, warehouse, shop or bank manager, and sometimes is, though in practice many of us still have the atavistic feeling that the farmer is the producer par excellence and that these others are somehow not so worthy. But why is our admiration justified? Because we see in the good husbandman how the ownership of property has produced in him a moral attitude to the bounty in his control, to those who cooperate with him in his activity, and to those who will acquire it and its increase after him. This applies to all property. Every time we treat it with care and diligence, we learn a lesson in morality. This is why the private ownership of property lends a moral dimension to the capitalist system. Contrast it with the treatment of so-called public property. No one needs to be told with what carelessness and lack of diligence most of us deal with it, whether in free or in communist countries. In fact, in communist countries the almost universally slack and dishonest treatment of communal property presents the rulers with one of their most intractable problems, and that despite the most painful and even barbarous penalties for transgressions.

There is another moral consequence of the attitudes engendered by private property, namely respect for the sanctity of contract. Sanctity of contract is one of the most important elements in the cement that binds a civilised society together. At the same time it has an elevating effect on man's character. It tends to arise naturally in a society that respects private property. *Verbum meum pactum* is the proud motto of the London Stock Exchange, an inner sanctum of capitalism, as its enemies, and perhaps some of its friends, envisage it. What more moral declaration is there than that 'My word is my bond'? With the growth of socialist ideas, policies and practices in the Western world, the belief in the sanctity of contract has crumbled away sadly and conspicuously. This is not the least of the evidences of moral decay in our society. Of course, it is easy to denigrate sanctity of contract when the creditor is malevolently pictured as a Shylock, demanding his pound of flesh. The truth is that a society that is guided by the morality of aggrieved debtors is on the way to disintegration.

The work ethic

A freshman student of economics who knows that 'there ain't no such thing as a free lunch', and why, has already gone far in the understanding of his subject. When Adam and Eve were expelled from Eden, the Lord said to Adam, 'By the sweat of thy brow shalt thou earn thy bread,' and this has been the human situation ever since. It is regarded as the curse of Adam, but in reality it is no curse. To know that, apart from a few blessings such as the air around us, nothing in this world is free, that everything has a cost that must be met, is a powerful agent of moral training. In a society rooted in individual responsibility, this is brought home to everyone. In a world of collectivism everything still has a cost, but the people are tempted, indeed to a large extent are urged, to behave as if the cost will be borne by someone else, usually the so-called 'rich'. The joke is then on the 'poor'. For it turns out that the taxes needed to meet the cost are levied on them as well as on the 'rich', and sometimes even more heavily owing to the incidence of sales taxes and the rules relating to the effect of income on welfare payments. At the same time, in a collectivised society the costs of everything are so jumbled up that nothing can be individually costed. This in itself tends to produce a tendency to act as if there really were such a thing as a free lunch.

Historically the work ethic is associated with the rise of capitalism, and has often been attributed to the impress on men's minds of Protestantism, especially in its Calvinist form. The truth, however, is that the work ethic can be seen to have been in operation wherever capitalism has been developed, including in Catholic and non-Calvinist Protestant areas. The difference was merely that it was given more explicit expression and a higher importance in Calvinist thought than in other religious teaching. Just as it is easy to sneer at respect for the sanctity of contract, so it is easy to sneer at the work ethic. The adherent of the work ethic is pictured as one who thinks of work as an end in itself, not as a means to the good life such as the use of leisure, the experience of pleasure, or contemplation. It is true that in the work ethic there is an element that regards work as good whatever it is devoted to, but it is not the same as believing that work is good in itself, though it looks like it. For even in such a case the work is regarded as good because it protects men against 'the Devil who finds work for idle hands to do'. The main basis of the work ethic is the same as that which produces the good husbandman. It is that we are in this world to make something of it and ourselves, and to leave it better than we found it.

Love thy neighbour

The moral training of property and the work ethic are important elements in the morality of the free economy. Yet they are far from the most important. Long ago we were told 'Thou shalt love the Lord thy God with all thy heart and with all thy soul and with all thy might and thy neighbour as thyself'. Whatever the colour of our religious beliefs or of our philosophical convictions, this is a prescription that is likely to command wide assent, even though we may not strive very hard to live up to it.

What does loving one's neighbour as oneself mean? It must mean that one wishes him to have what one most prizes for oneself. What do we most wish for ourselves? Is it a full belly, the secure provision of three meals a day? When people refer to compassion for others, they often talk as if this were so. Clearly it is not. A slave may have a full belly. A prisoner may have his regular three meals a day. So too may a soldier, but millions of young men would reject that as a reason for volunteering for the army. Of course, the starving man wants food before all else, and so would we if we were starving. But when we ask ourselves what we want above all else for ourselves, we do not picture ourselves to be starving. Is it then a secure roof over our heads, adequate clothing, or any other material benefits? Again we often talk as if this were the case. Once again, however, we know that these material goods may be available in slavery, in prison, or especially in the armed forces. When we say that we want them, we do so on a basic assumption, namely that we are free to seek them in accordance with our own freely chosen purposes.

This is the key to the commandment to love our neighbour. What we want above all for ourselves, and which therefore we must accord to our neighbour, is freedom to pursue our own purposes.

It is only when this is assumed that we talk about the primacy of food, clothing, shelter and any other material benefits and enjoyments. As a corollary of this freedom we want others to respect our individuality, our independence, and our status as responsible human beings. We do not want to be treated as children, not to mention slaves, or serfs, or prisoners, or conscripts, however generous or indulgent the treatment may be. This is the fundamental morality of the free economy and its great achievement. It alone among economic systems gives men the respect due to free, independent, responsible persons. All other systems in varying degrees treat men as less than this. Socialist systems above all treat men as pawns to be moved about by the authorities or as children to be given what the rulers decide is good for them, or as slaves to be chattels. For in all other systems the rulers act on the presumption that they know best. Therefore they are morally stunted. Only the free system, the much assailed capitalism, is morally mature.

Yet doubt may linger. Those who have been brought up on the Bible may say that surely one of the first lessons of the Bible is that we are, each one of us, our brother's keeper. They are mistaken, though their mistake has been given currency by many eminent men. When the Lord called upon Cain and said, 'Where is thy brother?' and Cain excused himself with the famous question 'Am I my brother's keeper?', the Lord did not say, 'Yes, thou art.' He simply said, 'Thy brother's blood cries out to me from the ground.' What Cain was doing was what slippery witnesses do every day in courts of law. They are asked a plain but incriminating question, and they answer with another question which is off the point. I am not my brother's keeper. If I were, he would be subordinate to me, as a child is to his parent, who truly is his keeper. I cannot love my neighbour as myself if I make him subordinate to me. If

I do, I become responsible for him and I deprive him of his self-responsibility. But cannot we be keepers of each other? If this means simply that we should help each other in our need, we certainly can, and we have noted that such help has always been conspicuous in capitalist countries. But for this 'keeper' is hardly the right word. When we help each other, our aid must be free from any derogation from self-responsibility. This is consistent only with a system of freedom. Thus we return to the moral maturity and superiority of the capitalist system.

Forward to capitalism

Socialism is the expression of atavistic errors and superstitions. We have scrutinised the moral foundations of the free economy and found them to be incomparably superior to those of any rival system. Yet with occasional stumbles and retreats the Western world has been sliding down the anti-capitalist road for several generations. It has done so under the influence of ideas of truly remarkable shoddiness. As the late Ludwig von Mises said many years ago, the only way to conquer bad ideas is with good ideas. It is to be hoped that some of the ideas propounded here may aid that conquest. As the anti-capitalist slide has taken us far back from the levels of civilisation established by our forefathers under the influence of capitalism and its associated ideas, our battle cry is clear. It must be 'Forward to capitalism'.

8 INDIVIDUAL RESPONSIBILITY AND COMPETENCE
Peter King

Introduction
Responsibility and competence

In this essay I wish to look at the question 'Must I be responsible for my own actions?' In particular I shall look at how commentators such as Murray have suggested that state provision erodes personal responsibility.[1]

The notion of responsibility connects in turn to that of *competence*, in the sense that, generally speaking, one should assume that individuals are competent to determine their own interests and make *responsible* decisions aimed at achieving these interests.

The structural thesis and the growth of welfare

Murray, in his discussion of social policy in America, suggests that it was the 'discovery' of structural poverty in the early 1960s which led directly to the development of large-scale government welfare provision. If individuals were not capable of counter-weighing the structural imbalances of the system, the answer was to change or redesign the system. As a result, government took up the role of

---

1   Charles Murray, *Losing Ground: American Social Policy, 1950–1980,* Basic Books, New York, 1984; Charles Murray, *Charles Murray and the Underclass: The Developing Debate,* Institute of Economic Affairs, 1996.

ameliorating the effects of the structural imbalances in the American economy.[2]

This presupposition of structural imbalances that render certain people economically incapacitated is not restricted to American thinking on social policy. Such structural assumptions also underpin the redistributionist ethic of British welfare policy.[3]

The implication of this assumption is that those afflicted with poverty are in no way to blame for the position they are in. Poverty is the result of the actions of the system in general – of the operations of markets, etc. – and not of the victims' actions. Poverty is seen as embedded in the structure of society and not curable merely by economic growth. Now if poverty is intrinsic to the system there is little the individuals affected can do to lift themselves out of it. Accordingly, there is no such thing as the deserving or undeserving poor; there are merely the blameless victims of forces beyond their control.

Indeed, the very notion of applying judgements to the needs of individuals is deemed to be offensive. If poverty is caused by structural imbalances at the level of society, then individuals cannot be held responsible for their predicament. If they cannot earn a living, or they have an income significantly below what is deemed satisfactory, this is not to be seen as the result of indolence or poor decision-making, but of the way in which society has been biased against them. Thus being on welfare should not only be blame-free, but also guilt-free. Not only was it not the fault of those who now depend on welfare that they have come to do so, but they should also not feel guilty about their dependency. It is

---

2   Murray, *Charles Murray and the Underclass*, op. cit.

3   J. Hills, *The Future of Welfare: A Guide to the Debate,* rev. ed., Joseph Rowntree Foundation, 1997.

not thought proper to suggest that an individual's situation has arisen as a result of his or her own actions or omissions.

A British example of this approach is seen in Hills when he considers the future of welfare in this country.[4] Hills's discussion of welfare, and particularly his treatment of distribution issues, is rooted not in desert, but in demographics. The assumption is that a certain distribution of resources has arisen because of the particular nature of the British economy and society in general. The role of collectivised welfare is to deal with this structural imbalance, an imbalance that leaves certain individuals worse off than others. Certain groups of individuals are seen as incapable of changing their situation themselves because of structural barriers.

Murray's attack on the removal of responsibility

Murray's criticism of the structural perspective had been precisely that it had the effect of removing any sense of blame or responsibility from individuals for the situations in which they find themselves. He argued that individuals were not only capable of materially affecting their position, but that their ability to respond extended also to the state's attempts to ameliorate their poverty. Thus the policy aimed at altering the purported structural imbalances in the US economy actually created an incentive for those imbalances to grow. The very provision designed to prevent a particular social malaise in reality encouraged its growth because there was now some economic advantage in occupying a particular social position identified as adverse.

Murray held specifically that the increase in poverty recorded

4   ibid.

in the USA since the early 1960s was a direct response to the introduction of measures aimed at relieving poverty. Individuals rationally altered their behaviour to maximise their income and benefits from state-funded programmes. Thus the provision of financial aid to lone parents had encouraged women to live separately from their partners and not to work because to do either of these things would lead to a loss of benefits.

The wisdom of assuming that individuals are competent and responsible

It would in general terms seem wise for us to assume that individuals are competent. It is true that this paves the way for the rejoinder that some individuals quite clearly are not. Indeed, some individuals, because of mental disability, are not capable of deciding for themselves.

My premise, however, is to suggest that there ought to be a general presumption of competence, rather than the counter-presumption that individuals are not competent and need government support. There will inevitably be individuals who are not able to determine their own interests, but these will be exceptional and readily identifiable. There is no necessary difficulty in meeting the needs of these people as exceptions. It would be possible to support these individuals – assuming they are not already part of a competent household – without a standardised national system of welfare incapable of identifying individual welfare needs. A general presumption of competence, far from being callous, would seek to enable individuals to get on with their lives instead of simply providing for them.

The presumptions of general competence and free choice

In any case it is necessary to make a distinction between those able to *choose* how to fulfil their needs and those who genuinely cannot. With respect to most human actions it would seem reasonable to presume the existence of a degree of voluntarism, that is to say that the actors knew and willed what they did. From this presumption that individuals are competent and know their own interests, there would follow the general inference that individuals' predicaments have often arisen as a result of their own actions: they have chosen to be where they are.[5]

This is a position diametrically opposed to the structural argument, which sees individuals as hemmed in by forces beyond their control. Rather than viewing individuals as passive victims of impersonal social forces, this perspective sees them as responsible, rights-bearing agents capable of taking decisions. This capability may be constrained by factors beyond their control. Individuals may be made involuntarily unemployed, but this does not mean that they do not have any choices. They can retrain, move to another area, take low-paid jobs, or decide to survive on state benefits until the right offer comes along.

Similarly, the overwhelming majority of pregnancies arise from voluntary acts between consenting adults. Most couples are aware of the potential consequences of sexual behaviour and therefore can properly be said to have chosen a particular route. There are exceptions to this, such as rape and incest, but these again should not be the models from which general policies are derived, precisely because they *are* exceptional.

---

5   This is not at all to deny that accidents and misfortunes not of their own doing happen to people.

The aim is not censoriousness but the call to responsibility

The aim here is not to be censorious and try to prescribe certain actions, but simply to assert the belief that individuals are capable of determining their own interests and how they go about achieving them. It is a matter for personal choice whether an individual takes a particular job or whether a couple decides to have a child. This should imply that no one else should bear the responsibility for that action. If individuals are competent and capable of determining their own needs, it follows that they should be held to account for the consequences of their actions.

Choices have consequences and this instrumentality is unavoidable. At times, however, social policy, in its refusal to apportion blame, seeks to move the responsibility for these consequences on to the state. But this leads to precisely the problem Murray identified in his 'Law of Unintended Rewards'. Murray argued that 'Any social transfer increases the net value of being in the condition that prompted the transfer.'[6]

Murray's purpose here is not to suggest that certain households should not be helped, but rather to suggest that a social policy whose ideological colouring is 'blame-free' has had disastrous consequences for personal responsibility and for the role of the state. It has perpetuated the view that individual actions are free of any personal consequences and has placed that burden on the state. As a result, irresponsibility has grown along with dependency. *Indeed, these are really two words describing the same condition.*

---

6 Murray, *Losing Ground*, op. cit., p. 212.

Communitarianism

The issue of personal responsibility is now firmly on the political agenda. This is seen by some as a reaction against the supposed individualism of the 1980s and early 1990s, which placed individual rights over responsibility to the community.[7] Communitarian writers have argued that social and economic libertarianism has created an atomistic culture in which social institutions are collapsing. They see issues such as anti-social behaviour and a reluctance to work as examples of this and attempt to devise social and public policies that will re-create the lost sense of community or civic order. Their argument is that individuals have a responsibility to others and that the role of the state is to ensure that this is maintained. While this sense of solidarity and responsibility was also present in more old-fashioned collectivist views, the different emphasis that communitarianism brings to the debate is the clear contention that *individuals* have a responsibility to others. Thus the concentration is not so much on state provision of needs, but on ensuring that individuals act in a responsible way, it being possible, according to communitarians, to ascertain what the proper way to behave is. We can see some of these ideas taking effect today in housing administration, with such policies as strong discouragement of anti-social behaviour and the use of probationary tenancies. Individuals are 'encouraged' to act in certain ways on pain of sanction.

The implication here is that it is possible to determine the 'cor-

7   D. Bell, *Communitarianism and Its Critics*, Clarendon Press, Oxford, 1993; A. Etzioni, *The Spirit of Community: Rights, Responsibilities and the Communitarian Agenda*, Fontana, London, 1993; J. Sacks, *The Politics of Hope*, Jonathan Cape, London, 1997; D. Selbourne, *The Principle of Duty: An Essay on the Foundations of the Civic Order*, Sinclair-Stevenson, London, 1994.

rect' way to behave. Moreover, there is an assumption that government has a legitimate role in correcting any behaviour that does not meet the required standard. This means that punitive action is taken against certain individuals and groups, at the same time, as we have seen, as other forms of behaviour are tolerated and even encouraged by government policy. It also means that, despite a rhetoric of individual responsibility, the role of government remains central. Government is assumed to be acting on behalf of the community and its values.

It is reasonable to propose that the state should be neutral towards its citizens, whom it has a duty to protect equally.[8] It is not for the state arbitrarily to apportion benefits for some and punishments for others. Punishments are appropriate only in response to coercion and violation of the rights of others. The problem for the citizen is that there is no recourse beyond the state itself, and so the citizen is left without protection.

Individualist responsibility

An individualist approach to responsibility would be to reject the notion that one can always state an objective notion of the public good or the needs of the community. Rather, one should take a personal responsibility for oneself and for others because of the mutual constraints placed upon us for each person to protect the interests of others.[9] This means that my recognition of the rights of others is grounded in their recognition of mine. The ends of diverse individuals may be incommensurable and this may mean

---

8   P. King, 'Housing, Equality and Neutrality', *Journal of Housing and the Built Environment*, 15(2), 2000, pp. 115–30.

9   R. Nozick, *Anarchy, State and Utopia*, Blackwell, Oxford, 1974.

that the rights of individuals will be in conflict.[10] These rights cannot be overridden by force or arbitrary government, however, but only set aside by *voluntary agreement* through public discussion and compromise. Certain acts, such as paedophilia, theft, violence and murder, are quite clearly infringements of the rights of others and require punitive action by the state. Legitimate disputes about lifestyles and choices, by contrast, are not. The role of the state in these latter cases is to be a neutral upholder of certain agreed abstract and general principles, not to take sides in terms of what behaviour is acceptable and what is not.

This is by no means to suggest that 'anything goes', or that certain forms of behaviour ought to be permitted unchallenged. But in a free society it is not for the state to adjudicate between rival views of the good life and to interpose in the choices that competent individuals make. On the other hand, it is not for the state to shield individuals from the consequences of their actions. If individuals are competent, as mostly they are, they should take responsibility for their actions.

It is true that the effects of such an outlook would be quite far-reaching in terms of social policy and the expectations of many people currently dependent on welfare services. It is also the case that what has been outlined above is an ideal position, which would have to be hedged around with caveats to deal with particular situations that might arise. Even so, as a general principle – that individuals are competent and capable of taking responsibility for their actions – it can form the basis of a root-and-branch reform of welfare services, including housing provision.

---

10   I. Berlin, *Four Essays on Liberty*, Oxford University Press, 1969.

9 MARKETS, THE INTERNET AND MORALITY
Sean Gabb

Introduction

The purpose of this essay is to explore the connections that exist – or are coming to exist – between the Internet and moral life. I want to argue that the Internet, far from tempting us to wrongful acts and enabling our immorality, is in fact the greatest means that our age possesses of upholding morality as it should be rightly understood.

For some this will doubtless seem a peculiar assertion. The Internet, we are often led to believe, is all about hacking, software and other copyright piracy, pornography, National Socialist propaganda, bomb-making recipes, and just about everything else that people regard as bad. The assertion can, nevertheless, be defended. First, however, let us turn to the preliminary issues of the nature and development of the Internet.

What is the Internet?

The Internet is a collection throughout the world of very powerful computers ('hosts') *connected to the telephone network*. These in turn are connected to smaller computers ('users') in homes. Electronic messages can be sent between these computers, whether in travelling businesses, government offices, libraries or places of education, either directly from host to host or indirectly via any number of other hosts, depending on how congested the whole network happens to be. It is also possible to retrieve documents and other items stored on the hard disks of computers permanently connected to the Internet.

The Internet emerged in the late 1960s, overlooked by the rest of the world, as a means of moving large amounts of information within the American defence establishment. During the 1970s and 1980s, it grew rapidly but still unnoticed by all but those involved in its growth. By the 1980s, universities had become the main agents of expansion. They were joined by large companies and a number of privileged private users. In 1982, the number of hosts reached 200. By 1983, this had grown to 500. In 1984, it reached 1,000, in 1986 5,000, in 1987 10,000, by 1988 60,000, by 1989 100,000, and in 1991 600,000. Most of these were based in the USA, though perhaps 10 per cent were in countries such as Britain, Germany and Japan.

It was around this time that the US military abandoned the Internet as a primary means of communication. With the end of the cold war and the improvement in other kinds of telecommunications, the Internet as it had developed was no longer needed. At this point, it was a much smaller version of what it is today – a collection of hosts and users spread around the world.

For a few years longer, though, its general use was retarded by a lack of computing power. Personal computers had been available since the late 1970s; but it was only in 1993, with the Pentium I processor, that they became capable of running Internet software that could be generally understood. Then there was the speed of modem connections. As late as 1991, the standard speed was still only 2,600 bits per second, compared with the present standard of 56,000 bits per second.

The world online

For want of any better alternative date, the world went online in March 1994, when the first version of the Netscape browser was released. From then on the Internet seemed to explode. The statistics showing the number of new users do not really describe the impact of what has happened since. Politics, business, shopping, personal relationships – all have been transformed by the Internet. Millions of intense friendships have come into being between people who have never been less than a thousand miles distant from each other. Every large organisation has a website, as do an increasing number of smaller ones. Newspapers must compete with Internet discussion lists and newsgroups as sources of information. Perhaps more significantly, the authorities in all countries are aghast at the opportunities for unregulated and often unknowable communication between people, and are hovering nervously between trying to censor the Internet and trying to use it to their own advantage. It took 50 years for the telephone to progress from an interesting toy to a standard means of communication. It took less than five years for the Internet to be taken up by almost everyone interested in communicating with the rest of the world. Many of us already have trouble recalling how we ever managed without it.

The Internet and the moral order

Now, what has all this to do with morality? How is it that people who log on to the Internet to buy airline tickets, or look at smutty pictures, or exchange complaints about the European Union or vivisection or the illiteracy of advertising copywriters or whatever – how is it that by running up our telephone bills and ignoring our loved ones we are advancing the cause of morality? There are three answers, one indirect, the other two very direct.

An indirect source of moral improvement: the attenuation of market imperfection

First, there is the avoidance of market failure. For over a century, neo-classical economics has involved the analysis of allocative efficiency. This is an alleged state of economically rational equilibrium, derived from a number of variously unrealistic assumptions about the world. On the one side, the perfectly competitive model assumes perfectly rational consumers. On the other side, we have profit-maximising firms operating in perfectly competitive markets. All products are similar enough for them to sell on price alone rather than any considerations of brand loyalty. All information regarding prices and technical possibilities is freely available to all players. There is easy entry into and exit from all markets. Goods, labour and capital are all freely mobile within and between markets.

Given these assumptions, unhampered demand and supply will bring about the best possible use of available resources – 'best possible' being defined as the satisfaction of consumer desires as expressed in the marketplace. In such a world, a structure of production will emerge, any departure from which will diminish the aggregate economic welfare of the society in which it exists.

This theorising is evidently unrealistic. Consumers are not perfectly rational. Not only do they fail to analyse their preferences but they are ignorant of all but a few alternative products and prices. Nor are many markets perfectly competitive. Markets are often dominated by a few buyers or sellers. Imperfect knowledge means that most purchases are made – albeit loosely – according to brand loyalty, and superior alternative products do not always easily make their way. New production methods are routinely monopolised, either kept secret or patented. Moreover, even if all the required information were available, it would date within seconds, as consumers changed their preferences and new products or new production methods were discovered. Economic reality, as the Austrian school has always asserted, is a very imperfect distribution of economic knowledge.

The value of the Internet is that it makes some of the assumptions of neo-classical economics more realistic. It does this by making information more cheaply and readily available. It lets both buyers and sellers make themselves and their preferences known to a much larger part of at least the consumer goods market than has ever before been possible. Local monopolies and other imperfections which exist through ignorance or distance or inertia are being undermined as the world becomes a single market. This means a downward homogenising of prices of all affected products.

There are markets that intensify traditional market functions and there also are wholly new markets

Obviously, traditional companies are working hard on getting their websites fitted out with all the latest facilities for demonstrating and selling their products. But there are more innovative and interesting approaches to e-commerce, and these may be among the successful business models of the future. A number of examples are described below.

There are auctions – via Amazon.com, eBay, Yahoo and hundreds of sites specialising in everything from collector coins to industrial supplies. Online auctions may be the most successful and efficient new marketplaces on the Internet. They have been taken up enthusiastically by both buyers and sellers. eBay has signed up over 10 million people, and other auction sites have also grown rapidly in the past few years.

There are 'name your price' auctions – via Priceline.com and Microsoft Expedia, among others. Here, buyers say how much they will pay for goods or services. Sellers can choose whether or not to offer at those prices. This is particularly useful for selling otherwise unwanted airline tickets and hotel bookings. Attempts are being made to sell cars and groceries as well.

There are innovations in the tradition of group buying – via Mercata.com and Accompany.com, among others. This has become commonplace, with groups of people looking for the same product coming together from all over the world and negotiating group deals with suppliers, often at a substantial discount. There is nothing new in this. Trade unions have long been negotiating group deals for their members in insurance and other products. What makes this different is that people are able to come together in temporary combinations that exist for the sole purpose of getting the sort of discount that was once available only to large organisations.

Buyer-driven markets have become more notable than ever – via Imandi.com, Respond.com, iWant.com and eWanted.com, among others. These function to let buyers advertise what goods or services they want, and then to let sellers compete to supply them.

There are product reviewers – via CNET, Epinions.com, Productopia and Deja.com, among others. These give shoppers product recommendations and reviews so they can make wise buying decisions.

Meaningful morality implies choice and wider markets mean wider choice, including moral choice

It may be asked what all this lengthy recitation has to do with morality. How does the ability to find the cheapest second-hand Ford Mondeo in the world make us better people? The answer is that if morality is to mean anything, it must involve choice. Suppose, for example, a man is forced at gunpoint to feed the starving. This may relieve hunger, but he has not performed a moral act. Equally, if he gives poisoned bread to a hungry person, and owing to some constitutional oddity the person is nourished by it, the donor has not performed a moral act. The morality of an act lies not solely in the act itself, but also in the intention behind it. To be good we must want to do good. An absence of good intention or the presence of ill intention both rob any act of its moral value. To say otherwise leads us to absurdity. It would be like calling the rain a moral force if it put out a fire, or accusing spiders of immorality for spinning cobwebs in places hard to clean.

The most moral social order is thus one that enables the fullest possible scope for freedom of choice. A social order that minimised or abolished this capacity might compel any number of convenient acts, and put down any number of inconvenient ones, but not one of them would have any moral significance. Give us, on the other hand, a society in which compulsion was minimised, and though it might contain fewer convenient acts, it would be immeasurably more moral. Where adultery is not a crime fidelity is a greater exercise of moral choice. For the same reason, people might virtuously choose to refrain from lying, or personal cowardice, or idleness, or spiteful gossip. So long as there is no compulsion used, these are fully moral choices. Introduce compulsion and the moral choice is ostensibly reduced or even eliminated. Humans become closer to mere animals or even things.

Freedom of choice is inseparable from private property

Freedom of choice is inseparable from the institution of private property. We can see this most clearly in the case of charity. As Margaret Thatcher once observed, when the Samaritan paused to save the man who had fallen among thieves, he had more than kind words to offer. He had wine and oil to pour into the wounds, and money to pay at the inn for a bed and other care. Before we can give, we must have. If we have not, we cannot give. If we take from others, or from a common stock, we give at best of whatever time is needed to take what others have produced.

We see this also in other moral acts, where individuals feel required by conscience to act against the settled opinion of society. The English campaigners who put down slavery were regarded at first as troublemakers. If all goods had been held in common and allocated according to the votes of the majority, or the will of a ruling elite, those campaigners would certainly have been forced back into conformity by the prospect, however distant, of starvation. It was because they had property, or were funded by others with property, that they had the practical freedom to do what they felt was right.

Private property, therefore, is what enables the free choice from which morality proceeds. Let us further accept the claim – generally accepted by economists and politicians – that market systems generate more wealth as they become more efficient, and we are then in a position to demonstrate the indirect moral implications of the Internet. So far as it improves the working of markets, reducing friction within them and bringing them even a little closer to the ideal of allocative efficiency, it is a force for good. Whoever, then, uses the Internet to buy a home-delivery pizza, or to make a free international telephone call, is not merely saving money, but also helping to make the world more moral. Why should not a form of salvation abide in such humble acts?

The morality of non-economic choice

Continuing this theme brings us to our second point. The Internet does not just enable choice, but is fundamentally *about* choice. There are people who complain about the large amounts of pornography available on the Internet, beyond the jurisdiction of any purely national set of laws. Let us assume for the sake of argument that looking at pornography is immoral, an assumption that I reject. Granting this, which is the more moral response: to pass laws that somehow make pornography unobtainable or to leave it to rational adults to decide for themselves what they will look at? In the light of what I have already said, my answer should be clear.

Morality lies in having the freedom to do wrong, but in then choosing what is right. Doubtless many people, even perhaps a majority, would prefer that there were no pornography in existence. Even if pornography were immoral, it is arguably more immoral to ban it than to allow it on the Internet, thereby giving people the ability to choose not to look at it. Arguments to the contrary at best confuse the question of the *sinful* with that of the criminal.

The same considerations apply to Internet material that nowadays raises rather stronger objections than portrayals of adult sexuality. Consider particularly incitements to racial hatred and arguments in favour of Holocaust revision, among much else.

The Internet as a moral force in the public sphere

The third point is that the Internet allows us to apply pressure to public figures to compel them to behave in what may be regarded as a more moral fashion. The pressure in question is *not* the positive legal force that moral authoritarians want to apply when they talk about making people good. What is implied here is the negative force of public disapproval, in this instance disapproval primed by the information made available over the Internet. We all have the right not to be harmed in our lives, liberty and property without due process of law – and with due process only on grounds that an educated, dispassionate observer would think just and reasonable. But no one has the right to make people employ him, or rent him property, or buy from him, or sell to him, or vote for him, or believe him. Undoubtedly, if these things are lost through the disapproval of others and their subsequent refusal to associate with him, a man loses perhaps as greatly and suffers perhaps as bitterly as if he had been thrown into prison. But in the case of prison, he has suffered a positive diminution in his rights – however justified that may be in the circumstances – whereas in the other case he is simply, by incurring the moral disapproval of members of the public, passed over consistently in favour of others, and by people who are exercising a peaceful dominion over their own lives, liberty and property. His personal autonomy of action is reduced because he has offended morally.

Moral autonomy and freedom are somewhat different things. Freedom in the classic liberal sense exists when there is no force or fraud used to influence action, whereas moral autonomy can be reduced by the disapproval of others or augmented by their approbation. It is very regrettable when public disapproval is strong enough and fierce enough to stop private individuals from doing things that do not cause harm to others as reasonably defined. Even so, complaints about the supposed tyranny of public opinion are probably exaggerated. Let people be free to act in private, or let there be a wide range of alternative employments and a diversity of neighbourhoods, and this tyranny is moderated where not prevented. The real targets of public disapproval are those who have, for whatever reason, put themselves into the public domain and offended subsequently by their proven inconsistency. These are the people who will most suffer from the glaring light of the Internet.

When moral pressure is legitimate

Let us suppose, for example, that a businessman takes care to have himself portrayed as a decent person, but is really giving support to some policy that is in the highest degree injurious in exchange for monetary favours and social recognition. Or let us suppose that a politician gives what seems a definite promise to advance the public good, but has, through verbal trickery or a simple disregard for the truth, decided to do the opposite once he has gathered in the votes. Or suppose a newspaper owner makes a display of his regard for the truth, but is really using his position to spread lies or disinformation.

These people are behaving immorally. To some extent, it may reduce their moral autonomy if they find that their immoral behaviour is open to discovery and legal punishment. But their status rests on the approval of others; and they have deliberately set out to obtain this status and then to retain it on fraudulent grounds. To discover their behaviour and punish them for it is different in nature from sacking a shop assistant because he is not orthodox in his opinions on, say, the question of immigration. When they make claims to public approval, the grounds on which they claim approval become matters of legitimate public concern. And the Internet is useful here for such claims to be investigated and for such concern to be expressed.

The media reborn

The established media no longer perform this salutary function. The Internet, however, does promise to take it over. It promises a return to freedom of speech on matters of public importance. It means freedom for public opinion to be reborn as it used to exist before about 1910. Since then in Britain the media has at least distorted the news. Instead of reflecting what people are really thinking, and reporting what the politicians are really doing, it has created a world close enough in appearances to the real one not to cause scandal, but in which nearly all the substance has been replaced. It does this by a subtle yet effective framing of arguments, by turns of phrase, by terminology.

It seems paranoid to say this in a country where no laws exist against propagating any point of view, but the issues are presented by the British media in ways that often prevent their being intelligently discussed. Part of this, no doubt, proceeds from the nature of those who tend to seek employment in the media. Part of it, though, is the effect of a centralised media, the owners of which have been co-opted into the Establishment.

The Internet is changing this. The West is moving perceptibly into an age of zero censorship. We are not there yet – not even in the USA, where the revolution is most advanced. But it is plain where we are heading. The intricate web of laws and informal pressures that governs expression even in the freest countries is being broken through. If we want to publish unorthodox opinions, we no longer need to negotiate with editors, hoping at best for a letter to be published or to be laughed at even while one is allowed on to a current affairs programme. If we want to read such opinions, we no longer need to hunt down obscure little pamphlets and newsletters. It is increasingly irrelevant whether the media barons are offered bribes or threatened with prison: their ability to manipulate what we read or see or hear is withering almost by the day. If still only in small amounts, everything is now available on the Internet, and can be accessed as easily as looking for a Chinese takeaway in the Yellow Pages. And every day, more pages are created on the World Wide Web, and more data flows through the newsgroups.

We are increasingly in a position to know what is happening, and to make our opinions about this directly available to millions of other people. So far as this promotes the cause of truth, and prevents those who seek our trust from abusing it, we are moving not just into an age where pornography and hate are freely available, but into a better and a more moral world.

This may read like an uneasy combination of technological utopianism and semi-scholastic moralising. Perhaps, then, I should close my argument with a quotation from someone who always knew exactly what he wanted to say and how to say it well. In his *Areopagitica* of 1644, John Milton argued thus for the cause of morality and unlicensed printing:

> [W]hat wisdome can there be to choose, what continence
> to forbeare without the knowledge of evill? He that can
> apprehend and consider vice with all her baits and seeming
> pleasures, and yet abstain, and yet distinguish, and yet
> prefer that which is truly better, he is the true wayfaring

> Christian. I cannot praise a fugitive and cloister'd vertue,
> unexercis'd and unbreath'd, that never sallies out and
> sees her adversary, but slinks out of the race, where that
> immortal garland is to be run for not without much heat
> and dust.

A closing note in troubled times

In the early twenty-first century, the most noteworthy fact about the Internet was the failure or extreme underperformance of many of its leading companies. This, however, will promote a short-term disturbance to a generally rising trend. Just as with the railway boom of the 1840s, short-term embarrassment should not disguise from anyone that we are in a period of rapid, unpredictable and probably irreversible change. Not least among the aspects of this change will be the pressure brought by the Internet on public figures to behave with greater moral consistency.

10 CAPITALISM AND CORRUPTION: THE ANATOMY OF A MYTH
Dennis O'Keeffe

Introduction
The idea that wealth leads to immorality is ancient

The notion that the ownership and pursuit of wealth lead to moral corruption reaches back across the history of civilisation. It is interesting that the consequences of property and affluence have typically been seen in this adverse light. Today, the governing view among intellectuals, at least in social science and the humanities, is still that private wealth is more productive of moral ill than moral good.

It is strange that the very powerful moral and intellectual case that can be put, both for the operations of markets in general and for the acquisition of wealth in particular, so often goes by the board. Some modest redress is attempted here.

The intellectual classes are the villains of the piece. Today, when a minority of their kind, and the majority of the human race, regard markets as overwhelmingly slanted towards human felicity, most academics in the theoretical and applied social sciences remain obstinately stuck in socialism's moralistic time warp. Fortunately, they are not very representative of humanity and their opinion has not stopped the search for wealth being normalised in the rapidly growing free world. Nor has it in those societies where markets are 'free', even when political systems are not. Where the market writ runs, more or less, the main achievement of the socialist intelligentsia is to have compromised and inhibited markets, not to have frustrated them totally.

Wealthy societies would be even richer but for mischievous socialist opinion

A crude but effective way of putting this is to say that already very rich societies like ours would be even richer but for mischief-making socialist opinion. While most people in the advanced societies today are unimaginably richer than people in past centuries, the prejudice against wealth may well prevent the differences being even greater. Resources that could go into real wealth formation are, for example, sometimes squandered on the welfare state or, as Peter Bauer suggested, on trying to exploit the political process to change resource allocation in favour of or obtain rents for particular interest groups.

Markets: vicious, virtuous or neutral?

The question of the moral nature of markets may be discussed either in religious or secular terms. The central concern here is secular, although the religious aspect will be touched on. In both cases there are three main, broad possibilities:

1 The operations of the market in engendering profits and wealth are morally corrupted and corrupting.
2 These operations are morally neutral.
3 They are morally virtuous.

These three categories can be much nuanced. Wealth may be thought differentially corrupting or improving. It may be seen as having neutral outcomes for most people but not for others, some being corrupted or improved by it. Scale may count too. Some thinking will hold modest fortunes to be sound but baulk at huge ones. Indeed, throughout the ages it has mostly been great wealth, rather than typically modest wealth, which has been linked with moral ill. Periodic ascetics have fulminated against all wealth, all materialism. Marxism is rather different, welcoming wealth roundly, provided only that it is socialist wealth, a phrase we may be tempted to regard as oxymoronic. Clearly, there are many possible variations. We are concerned, however, with the general tendencies of the case.

Positive and normative economic theory
From Marxism to neo-Marxism

Let us consider, very tersely, the principal positive and moral perspectives of the main economic schools. All have positive and normative positions, though not in equal incidence. For classical Marxism, under capitalism all economic agents will, effectively, attempt to maximise their wealth/income. Oddly, only one group, the capitalists, is singled out for moral censure in this regard. Strictly speaking, the analysis fixes on the capitalist class's allegedly self-defeating search for ever greater profits. Since, however, the workers are seen as locked in inexorable class struggle with the bourgeoisie, by implication they too are engaged in income maximisation.

In fact classical Marxist economics has been abandoned by today's 'radicals'. Profit maximisation does not apply to neo-

Marxism, which assumes that economic agents often engage in the irrational (in profit terms) pursuit of racial and sexual prejudice.[1] All forms of Marxisms, however, involve heavy doses of normative criticism within the putative science. Indeed, they are far more moralistic than their rivals. The real meat of the case is 'exploitation' and 'alienation'.

Today's anti-capitalism is residual

It is proper to have mentioned Marxism first of all. Since the rise of Marxism in the nineteenth century, it has shouldered almost all the theoretical case against the market. Now classical Marxism has largely collapsed. Indeed, it is probable that most of today's radical intellectuals would not even call themselves 'neo-Marxist'. Yet the ancient prejudices Marx inherited, theorised and popularised have not perished, though no new general theory has emerged to theorise them again. Today's anti-capitalism is thus residual and rather atheoretical in character. A moral critique once articulated via a *wrong* theory now has virtually no elaborate theoretical backing.

Neo-classicism and Keynesianism

Neo-classicism, the most rationalist of paradigms, says that we are all maximisers, but not necessarily of wealth or income. It may be

---

1   There is a vast literature; but see, for example, the volte-face performed by Samuel Bowles and Herbert Gintis, as between their virtually communist tract of the mid-seventies, *Schooling in Capitalist America* (Routledge and Kegan Paul, London, 1976), and their feeble rightsology in *Democracy and Capitalism: Property, Community and the Contradictions of Modern Social Thought* (Routledge and Kegan Paul, London, 1986).

power or prestige we pursue. Neo-classicism is often seen as justifying markets, though it lacks much formal normative underpinning. Long ago, J. B. Clark did argue, on the basis of marginal productivity theory, that under competition, each contributor receives the morally just valuation of his contribution.[2] On the whole, however, neo-classicists have gone in for a *sotto voce* moral assumption of the superiority of capitalism rather than explicit moral celebration of markets, etc. This is indeed also true of most mainstream economic theorising. The explicit praise sung of markets has lauded their efficiency rather than their virtue.[3]

Keynesianism is not very moralistic, though it famously holds unemployment to be an obvious evil. Positively, its status is unsettled. Believers still abound; but there are other scholars who regard it as no longer workable, such as Robert Skidelsky.[4] Marxists once excoriated it as a repair job for capitalism. It is also suspect in some quarters on mixed positive and normative grounds, associated as it is with inflation. Keynes himself, wrong or right, positively or normatively, did *not* regard markets and profits as immoral.

Austrian theorising

The Austrian approach is different again. It does not need to

---

2   J. B. Clark, *The Distribution of Wealth, A Theory of Wages, Interest and Profits*, New York, 1908 (quoted in Israel M. Kirzner, 'Some Ethical Implications for Capitalism of the Socialist Calculation Debate', in Paul *et al.* (eds), *Capitalism*, Blackwell, Oxford, 1989).

3   Paul Samuelson, *Economics*, McGraw-Hill, multiple edns. Samuelson is making a technical case, though the note of normative celebration is also clear when he asserts that the 'consumer is king'.

4   Back in the 1970s, at the start of his well-received biographical work on Keynes, Skidelsky told me of his interest in the question as to why the Keynesian synthesis no longer worked.

assume that economic agents are maximisers of any economic desideratum. Nor is its history much burdened with moral assertions as to the superiority of free enterprise. It is an economics, even a sociology of knowledge, arguing that the dispersed, never-to-be-comprehensively-grasped nature of economic knowledge makes socialism impossible as a system and (anti-socialist) neo-classicism invalid as a theory. Interestingly, however, one leading exponent, Israel Kirzner, has proposed that the Austrian view of profit-seeking sustains a sturdy implicit moral defence of markets.[5] Capitalism is moral because its dynamics depend on the discovery of profitable openings. Only if the activities concerned were intrinsically immoral could this discovery process be thought in any sense wrong. Discovery, that is to say the *finding* of unowned profit potential, in most circumstances justifies the finder in retaining these possibilities – 'finders keepers', in the old phrase.[6]

Economics, it seems, has nothing morally definitive to say on its subject matter. Marxisms seem enormously more moralistic than their rivals. There are supporters of free enterprise who maintain the clear superiority of markets; but the tone is not the relentless harrying one finds in socialist writings. On the positive front, let us allow for purposes of preliminary analysis that many capitalists *and* employees will seek to increase their wealth and income, maximally or not. Others, immorally, morally or neutrally, may be less interested in wealth than in 'rents' such as power, status and leisure.

---

5   Kirzner, op. cit., p. 176.
6   Professor Kirzner's extensive essay in the present volume is much more forthrightly assertive of the enlightened morality of capitalism.

The 'markets are immoral' case

Of the three versions of the capitalist/morality nexus, listed above, the first, that wealth endangers moral health, is the best known. Though it is foreign to the way so many of us live, though it lacks any elaborated theory many economists would accept, we must consider it. Are public morals adversely affected by the institutions and activities of the market?

This is the 'money is the root of all evil' theme, the age-old legend of filthy lucre, itself older than, but the same in essence as, Marx's contention that 'private property epitomises the evils of capitalism'. Marx went notably farther. The mere operation of market exchange induces alienation – commodity fetishism, etc.

The secular moral argument against free enterprise is that the search for wealth does, indeed, come mainly from this deeply tainted source. Thus the present essay may be seen as a part of our long-standing debate with Marx's ghost and the ghosts of his older inspirers, most of whose very names are lost. Marxism is ambiguous, hence questionable, because it hangs so cunningly between 'science' and morals. The disingenuous strain in the critique consists in its manifest appeal to allegedly scientific, neutral criteria, camouflaging a latent call to moral judgement and political action.

Marxist theory and practice have had disastrous effects

The results have been material and moral disaster. It has not mattered much in practice whether the opponents of the bourgeois economy have held it to be wrong because it is positively doomed or doomed because it is normatively wrong. Hundreds of millions have suffered and died from the errors of Marx, whether those errors are positive or normative. Indeed, as a source of evil Marxism's critique of private property, profit-oriented markets and the money economy surpasses all the rest of history's dire ideologies.[7]

One does not necessarily, therefore, have to endorse George Gilder's contention that markets are essentially virtue-provoking and that the entrepreneur is a virtuous figure.[8] The first reply to the Marxist critique is to look at the moral outcomes flowing from the institutionalisation of the Marxist counterfactual. There are, it seems, no significant dimensions of corruption that are not worse in the case of Marxist socialism than in the case of private enterprise. This is attested by a vast literature. Whatever ills may inhere in capitalism, then, are not to be removed or improved, indeed quite the contrary, by the full-blown socialisation of the economy.[9]

Anti-capitalists today do not seek to replace the whole market economy

This is not, however, fatal to the anti-capitalist moral critique. The case against free enterprise could still hold, even when the latter's general replacement by socialism has moral results that are clearly worse. There are, indeed, few writers today who will give unreconstructed Marxism much credence. There is little desire among

---

7   I am not entering the debate as to whether monstrous Hitler was worse than monstrous Stalin. In any case I take Hitler at his word and regard him as a socialist. On a sheer headcount basis Marxism breaks all records for murder. There is a vast literature. For a brilliant account of the murder and mayhem just in the early years of the Soviet Union, see Richard Pipes, *Russia under the Bolshevik Regime, 1919–1924*, Harvill, London, 1994.

8   George Gilder, *Wealth and Poverty*, Basic Books, New York, 1981.

9   P. J. D. Wiles, *Economic Institutions Compared*, Blackwell, Oxford, 1976.

socialist intellectuals, as far as most of the economic structure is concerned, to eliminate private property or competitive markets wholesale. But, then, why should they want to? Hayek identified fiscal socialism as the new version of the socialist challenge to, and moral critique of, the market order.[10] Welfarism, funded from taxing private enterprise, has replaced nationalisation and central planning, now that the 'liberals', social democrats or socialists, as they variously call themselves, realise that this brings them all, or at least much, of the power they seek.

Their moral critique has not actually changed much. It has widened its scope, however. Today's critics of free enterprise advocate (and secure) not a socialist economy proper but a powerful and extended state, consisting among other things of huge socialist sectors. This, they hold, will correct the various moral ills that they still believe the market engenders, such as unemployment and inequality, this latter now extended to take in such newly observed wrongs as the neglect of the old, the 'oppression' of women and non-whites, and even of homosexuals.

These moral critiques are not theorised in market terms, merely alleged

The notion that one could produce positive, scientific demonstrations of the specific market causes of these ills is scarcely broached. It is thus the normative side of the socialist critique which survives, indeed held still with a fanatical conviction, allied to the proposed or achieved hypertrophy of the state apparatus.

There is no widely agreed positive analysis. Despite the

---

10 Friedrich von Hayek, *The Constitution of Liberty*, Routledge, London, 1960.

diffuseness of the moral case, however, it is not without focus. British anti-Tories, for example, commonly assert that the 1980s, in particular, were associated with an explosion of human greed. This is a *central* part in the critique of 'Thatcherism'. A parallel tendency is apparent in the USA, in this case turning the moral blast in the direction of ex-President Reagan and his associates.

Few British socialists would reverse all privatisation. It is impossible politically and they probably do not want to anyway. They seek a large public sector, especially including the new 'commanding heights' (i.e. health, education and public welfare).[11] At the same time, 'greed' (large profits) is to be deplored and prevented.

The incoherent and promiscuous critique of 'greed'

Greed, known to moralists throughout history, has today resurfaced as a theme, indeed as a central plank, in the critical programme. Its castigators do not tell us how to identify and measure it, and proffer few suggestions on containing it, other than through punitive taxation. Senior management is castigated for its ruthless self-interest; but workable proposals as to how this 'greed' can be discouraged, other than through minatory controls, are not forthcoming. If all this does not sound very coherent, this is because it is not coherent, though it is more or less what the present Labour Party and government stand for, as does a fortiori the federalist tendency and its apparatus in Europe.

For all the muddle, the moral strain is not necessarily always wrong. Some capitalists, workers and sociology lecturers, for that

---

11   Dennis O'Keeffe, *Political Correctness and Public Finance*, Institute of Economic Affairs, London, 1999.

matter, *are* greedy. The argument fails, however, to relate this to markets. We already know that socialism makes a far worse moral hash of things. From those who castigate markets for greed come few hints on what exact mechanisms are at work, nor on what might rein the beast in – if it exists other than as a pyschological datum, a moral defect strongly present in some people and relatively absent in others – without destroying crucial economic incentives.

Loosely connected intellectually with greed – though the emotional bonds are tight – are the themes of resource depletion and ecological destruction. Here moralising nemesis is invoked on the basis of inadequate evidence.[12] Greed is thus a more functional rallying theme for the socialist cause. Perhaps it is precisely the fact that those who claim to discern it cannot conceptualise it properly, much less measure it, and that moves to attenuate it cannot safely be operationalised, which lends the theme such attraction.

The greed thesis is advisedly elastic

The greed motif works as a rallying cry, a kind of inspirational political metaphysic. It is hard to refute charges the substance of which is so elusive and which also appeal to decency. This serendipitous combination works to the advantage of residual socialism. Also, despite the death of Marxism proper, a kind of (also residual) materialist reductionism does survive. It is characteristically all purpose/all weathers. Various social ills are linked with the failure of the system – capitalism is lambasted as the cause of

---

12 There is no settled opinion on whether resources are running out or whether global warming is taking place or whether there is a hole in the ozone layer. These themes seem as precarious as 'greed'.

unemployment and crime explained as a consequence of this. By contrast the *success* of free enterprise is hugely underplayed at best and at worst dismissed as greed. This elasticity typifies an advisedly unfalsifiable thesis, whose advocates are not interested in the evidence and do not really want to destroy the system they castigate.

A developed economy permits most people to pursue economic advantage

In a developed economy the search for economic advantage becomes generalised. Most people pursue it, though 'it' may be leisure or power as much as wealth. The chase is not just for the bourgeoisie, either. Indeed, the patronising critique of 'Essex Man', a variant of 'capitalism leads to corruption', hits out more typically at high-income employees, e.g. of City firms, than capitalists proper. Ironically, the intelligentsia reserves its bitterest shafts for former proles who refuse to conform to type, who want conveniences that your average college lecturer will take for granted. The radical sociologist knows what is good for the prole, and it includes refraining from 'materialism'.

The moral ills of modernity relate more closely to the public than to the private sector

All this said, we remain assailed by moral ills: violence, theft, rape and the other wrongdoings of the human race. While residual socialism associates them with capitalism, it has produced remarkably little evidence of a connection. It is much more convincing to see them as perennial aspects of our wicked potential, liable to erupt when the controls are slackened. Concerning precisely that slackening, there is an alternative argument. Some of the manifest failings in our moral life today may be related precisely to the strange, sectoral socialism that has taken hold in the Western world. On this reckoning it is not markets which have evil effects, but their partial suppression by modern welfarism and state intervention.[13] It is to a brief consideration of this theme that we now turn.

The ills of sectoral socialism

The ills of socialist sectors in market economies have some resemblance to those of more ambitious versions of socialism. The mind-numbing scale of criminality of the Stalin, Hitler or Mao type is not there. It would be absurd to suggest it is. But, to parody Marx and Engels, let us note in wonder how many ills fester unnoticed in the bosom of public finance. The ills are well observed; but the public finance much less so. Crime and other social problems of the advanced world have little demonstrable connection with free enterprise.

The erosion of religion may be a large factor. The evidence is clearer on the secular front, where we find lax laws on divorce, and the spread of acutely egalitarian and antinomian ideas in social work, the probation services, teacher education and the study of the humanities. These are the sources of today's moral turpitude.

Many destructive ideologies are closely related to public spending. Many of them, for example progressive education or multi-

---

13   The classic work is Charles Murray's *Losing Ground*, Basic Books, New York, 1984. Murray does not, however, explain the problem along the lines of my argument.

culturalism, would not even get off the ground without public finance.[14] The moral reversals of recent decades bear little proven relation to free enterprise or markets. They flow from 'progressive', i.e. lax, social policies, driven by insidious ideologies often lavishly funded by the state. If there were a conspiracy against our moral order, a genuine desire to overthrow it definitively, the public agencies that teach men and women or whites and nonwhites to hate each other would be worth more to this cause than any number of corrupt millionaires.

The same would apply to the antinomian ideologies that have been pumped into social work, the probation service and teacher education. Even so unarguably a malign influence such as modern pop music should not be identified with capitalism as such. This and other social ills may be amplified by the activities of markets. Markets, in the classically neutral sense, may relay them on, but their origin is elsewhere. The unnoticed background to a moronic culture is a moronising school system.[15] The public sector interpenetrates the private. It gets its finance there. It buys its requirements there. Conversely, some private firms depend for their livelihood on purchases from the public sector. The two sectors are inextricably interpenetrated. But it is within the public sector that many of the ideas that tend to destabilise our society originate. On this crucially important theme there is virtually no think-piece writing and no empirical research at all.

14 O'Keeffe, op. cit.

15 Dennis O'Keeffe, 'The Philistine Trap', in Ralph Segalman (ed.), *Reclaiming the Family*, Paragon Press, 1998.

Are markets morally neutral?

In many circumstances not only are markets neutral but they have to be. There are no grounds, however, for the assumption that either buyers or sellers typically sin against each other. When Adam Smith said that we do not get our dinners through the benevolence of the butcher and the baker, he was not saying they are not benevolent, only that our trading is to their advantage and ours, rather than an act of charity on their part. They are neutral about us except in so far as we help them earn a profit: their primary concern with their own advantage cannot be met unless they think of ours. The stipulative decision of most modern socialists is that this entrepreneurial motive is often greed. We are justified, in the absence of decent evidence, in observing the arbitrary basis of this condemnation. The charge is simply wheeled out when it suits this or that purpose.

Altruism cannot minister to the world's economic needs

This kind of reasoning is faulty. The implied antonym of 'greed' here is altruism. Altruistic is what Smith's baker would have to be to avoid the charge of greed. It is hugely apparent that altruism cannot meet the world's economic needs.[16] Even if the view that profit-seeking necessarily corrupts people were well founded, such ill would still have to be accepted for the greater good. In the absence of substantial profit-making, most people in history were poor. In Africa today millions starve because not enough profit-making is going on. If all (or just quite a lot of)

---

16 Remove the profit motive from international production and millions of people would perish of starvation or in wars of international plunder.

profit-seeking were mere greed, then the world might indeed be said to need it.

In fact the view is *not* well founded. Israel Kirzner's essay in this present volume contends that it is widely, wrongly and dangerously believed today that our continued affluence does require the greed of capitalists.[17]

Moreover, in many circumstances well-intended generosity has manifestly disastrous results. This is true both of poor countries and of the poor in rich countries. Their plight may be rendered much worse by their long-term reliance on handouts.

Markets and prudential virtue

A commonsense view commends itself. Human nature is various and people differ enormously in their moral characters. Markets are in the main as good or as bad as those who use them. Some economic agents are corrupt and greedy. Some will cheat, lie and even murder to attain their ends. Such people are parasites on the decency or moral neutrality of the majority. There is no obvious reason to think them more readily to be found among capitalists than other people. Most profits, indeed most markets, depend on reliability and the keeping of promises. Without these, markets will break down and profits evaporate. In other words, markets typically influence the world at least in the direction of prudential virtue. Their typical effects belong at the decency end of the moral spectrum running from evil via neutrality to virtue.

---

17   Israel M. Kirzner, 'Economic Science and the Morality of Capitalism', p. 88.

Are markets virtuous?

It is quite a step from neutrality, mingled with prudential virtue, to grander moral good. Perhaps Gilder errs in his beatification of enterprise,[18] though Professor Marsland takes a comparable position in this volume.[19] Even to casual observation, however, it is apparent that the Armand Hammers of business are not typical. Many men and women, rich or otherwise, strive on behalf of their families. Many wish, commendably, to avoid becoming burdens on their fellows. Many capitalists are philanthropists on a vast scale. Indeed, the populations of the rich economies give generously to charitable causes, in what can be seen, additively, as praiseworthy collective morality. It is straining belief to dismiss love of family or care for one's fellows as mere prudential virtue, let alone as selfishness.

More important, though, is the moral life of ordinary economic existence. There is a good case for the view that private enterprise promotes freedom, reliability, tolerance and many other virtues. Private property has its moral perils; these are surely outweighed by its realised potential for human liberation. Private wealth promotes consensus, which is of inestimable value to the moral order. Since neolithic times most societies have relied on periodic brutal coercion to secure social control. This is not so in the advanced societies, where social control depends on a powerful value consensus, in which wealth, and perhaps even more the 'near-wealth' of human capital, plays an enormously important part. This consensus both demands and permits active private decision-making (including moral decisions) of an autonomous kind. This is to be

---

18   Gilder, op. cit.
19   David Marsland, 'Freedom and Virtue: The Social Structure of Morality', p. 101.

contrasted with the sullen passivity and dull habituation characterising social control in other social orders, including modern
socialism.[20]

Why we need markets

The worst immoralities of the last century were the work of the
state. Socialism drives the criminal element into politics. Dr John-
son is endlessly quoted here, because he is so incontestably right. A
man is never so innocently employed as when he is making money.
Just think what benefits Hitler or Stalin might have brought the
human race if their vast energies had been devoted to making profits. In free societies an Al Capone may become a criminal; but it
is quite possible that he will be able to sublimate his aggression
in money-making. In totalitarian societies, such a morally inferior
creature will make unerringly for a place in the political sun.

The grounds for markets are also overwhelming to anyone persuaded that living standards matter. It is also positively apparent
that we cannot have rich societies unless we have some very rich
people. This calls for markets uncompromised by the fanning up
of the forces of envy. It would be a strange morality, after all, which
secured the impoverishment of the many so that the relatively few
should not be very rich. Yet in so far as socialism has rested on
normative arguments, this is, indeed, one version of what happened in Russia after 1917; and in other communist societies after
World War II.

---

20 David Marsland, 'Human Capital and Stratification', in Dennis O'Keeffe *et al.*,
    Work, Employment and Class, Paragon, 1994.

Without the market and its associated apparatus, economic modernity is unattainable

The positive case is even more compelling. The socialist conceit that the benefits of modern technology can be passed to the human race without the mediation of a 'parasitic' market apparatus has proved disastrous. Markets are an integral part of modernity, without which life is not only diminished morally but rendered impossible positively. Whatever the precise impact on human morality of markets, they are indispensable.

Capitalism and peace

Acquisition may, we repeat, sublimate aggression. Without aggression the species would not advance. Cultural learning, however, is different from physical evolution, since the learning can be incorporated into social structures even when the human organism does not change.

Only the advanced capitalist economy is suitable for an aggressive species undergoing geometric technological evolution. This evolution now includes, for ever, the ability of the species to eradicate itself. If the rival superpower to Soviet Russia had been Nazi Germany, or maybe Maoist China, in direct struggle with the Soviets for world hegemony, what long-term chances of survival would the world have had? These were all societies where madness and depravity were in command.

There is no space for an extended treatment of the eirenic potential of the modern market economy. Some outline observations are worth making, however. First, the Marxist theory that the developed market economy is characterised by intense and ultimately dichotomous class conflict is provenly false. The evidence is quite to the contrary. One reason for favouring markets and the enterprise economy is their clear eirenic tendencies. The long-term trend of capitalism is to reduce conflict.

Nor is the standard neo-Marxist line that modern capitalism is essentially a war society upheld. On inspection, the advanced capitalist societies, though their governments may quarrel fiercely, seem radically indisposed to war among themselves. There is bellicosity in the advanced societies, but it is mostly vicariously indulged, either through sport and other entertainment or the TV observation of remote, high-tech warfare. Only rather rarely is it articulated by government.

The leisure pursuits (surrogate warfare) of many citizens may be morally obnoxious; but there is a kind of moral advance in the decline of the 'martial virtues'. There is a salutary side to the distaste for one's personal involvement in war. It is not always easy to separate this from flabby pacificism of the sort that sides with the free world's proven enemies. But since Vietnam, however shameful the West's vacillation then now appears, it is increasingly clear that the citizens of advanced capitalist societies are ill disposed to go to war.

By contrast, in societies that lack developed markets, either the sublimation of aggression, characteristic of advanced market systems, does not operate, or their denizens are not consulted. The world's need of more, not fewer, markets is witnessed in the dangers that menace us yet. Indeed, it could be argued that, in those countries where free trade is not the norm, war and the taking of the land and resources of others become a means of attempting economic advancement: advancement that morally, peacefully and more effectively comes from trade. In so far as the developed world is militarily threatened today from without, the threat, that

of real, as opposed to surrogate, war, comes from radical national-
ism and theocracy, or the after-effects of an increasingly residual
socialism. The internal threat comes from publicly funded anti-
nomianism.

A brief religious note

Both the Old and the New Testaments supply some grounds for
those who would criticise wealth in moral terms and who remain
deeply suspicious of the social as well as private effects of great
fortunes. Indeed, the word 'concupiscence', in the old theological
sense, refers not to sexual lust but to excessive desire for worldly
things. It has also to be said, however, that ambiguity reigns in this
area. The less well-known case is that Biblical texts abound which
at least imply that moral decency is perfectly consistent with great
wealth. The believing Christian who is also an advocate of free enterprise need not be dismayed by a one-sided emphasis on camels
too large for the eyes of needles.

The Bible does not furnish unambiguous grounds for the condemnation of wealth. Despite the humble circumstances of his
birth, Christ's family were evidently not poor; and both Testaments
have many examples of good people who were also very rich. Many
of the patriarchs, from Abraham to Isaiah, were wealthy. There is
no universal political economy that can be straightforwardly read
off the scriptures, a point that could not easily be gathered from
most of the recent socio-economic writings of British churchmen.

Indeed, to the Christian sociology that understands society
as a divine gift for the redemption of the human spirit there
can surely be added a contemporary economic rider. The developed market economy can be interpreted as a most notable

gift of Divine Providence. Like all such gifts it is capable of gross abuse, but in principle it offers a radical attenuation of the material conflicts that have raged across the ages, both within and between societies. The market militates against envy and covetousness precisely because it continues to free a growing proportion of the world's peoples from the ancient ravages of primary poverty, famine and disease.

ABOUT THE IEA

The Institute is a research and educational charity (No. CC 235 351), limited by guarantee. Its mission is to improve understanding of the fundamental institutions of a free society with particular reference to the role of markets in solving economic and social problems.

The IEA achieves its mission by:

- a high-quality publishing programme
- conferences, seminars, lectures and other events
- outreach to school and college students
- brokering media introductions and appearances

The IEA, which was established in 1955 by the late Sir Antony Fisher, is an educational charity, not a political organisation. It is independent of any political party or group and does not carry on activities intended to affect support for any political party or candidate in any election or referendum, or at any other time. It is financed by sales of publications, conference fees and voluntary donations.

In addition to its main series of publications the IEA also publishes a quarterly journal, *Economic Affairs*, and has two specialist programmes – Environment and Technology, and Education.

The IEA is aided in its work by a distinguished international Academic Advisory Council and an eminent panel of Honorary Fellows. Together with other academics, they review prospective IEA publications, their comments being passed on anonymously to authors. All IEA papers are therefore subject to the same rigorous independent refereeing process as used by leading academic journals.

IEA publications enjoy widespread classroom use and course adoptions in schools and universities. They are also sold throughout the world and often translated/reprinted.

Since 1974 the IEA has helped to create a world-wide network of 100 similar institutions in over 70 countries. They are all independent but share the IEA's mission.

Views expressed in the IEA's publications are those of the authors, not those of the Institute (which has no corporate view), its Managing Trustees, Academic Advisory Council members or senior staff.

Members of the Institute's Academic Advisory Council, Honorary Fellows, Trustees and Staff are listed on the following page.

The Institute gratefully acknowledges financial support for its publications programme and other work from a generous benefaction by the late Alec and Beryl Warren.

Other papers recently published by the IEA include:

WHO, What and Why?

Transnational Government, Legitimacy and the World Health Organization
Roger Scruton
Occasional Paper 113; ISBN 0 255 36487 3
£8.00

The World Turned Rightside Up

A New Trading Agenda for the Age of Globalisation
John C. Hulsman
Occasional Paper 114; ISBN 0 255 36495 4
£8.00

The Representation of Business in English Literature

Introduced and edited by Arthur Pollard
Readings 53; ISBN 0 255 36491 1
£12.00

Anti-Liberalism 2000

The Rise of New Millennium Collectivism
David Henderson
Occasional Paper 115; ISBN 0 255 36497 0
£7.50

Capitalism, Morality and Markets

Brian Griffiths, Robert A. Sirico, Norman Barry & Frank Field
Readings 54; ISBN 0 255 36496 2
£7.50

A Conversation with Harris and Seldon

Ralph Harris & Arthur Seldon
Occasional Paper 116; ISBN 0 255 36498 9
£7.50

Malaria and the DDT Story

Richard Tren & Roger Bate
Occasional Paper 117; ISBN 0 255 36499 7
£10.00

A Plea to Economists Who Favour Liberty: Assist the Everyman

Daniel B. Klein
Occasional Paper 118; ISBN 0 255 36501 2
£10.00

Waging the War of Ideas

John Blundell
Occasional Paper 119; ISBN 0 255 36500 4
£10.00

The Changing Fortunes of Economic Liberalism

Yesterday, Today and Tomorrow
David Henderson
Occasional Paper 105 (new edition); ISBN 0 255 36520 9
£12.50

The Global Education Industry

Lessons from Private Education in Developing Countries
James Tooley
Hobart Paper 141 (new edition); ISBN 0 255 36503 9
£12.50

Saving Our Streams

*The Role of the Anglers' Conservation Association in
Protecting English and Welsh Rivers*
Roger Bate
Research Monograph 53; ISBN 0 255 36494 6
£10.00

Better Off Out?

The Benefits or Costs of EU Membership
Brian Hindley & Martin Howe
Occasional Paper 99 (new edition); ISBN 0 255 36502 0
£10.00

Buckingham at 25

Freeing the Universities from State Control
Edited by James Tooley
Readings 55; ISBN 0 255 36512 8
£15.00

Lectures on Regulatory and Competition Policy

Irwin M. Stelzer
Occasional Paper 120; ISBN 0 255 36511 X
£12.50

Misguided Virtue

False Notions of Corporate Social Responsibility
David Henderson
Hobart Paper 142; ISBN 0 255 36510 1
£12.50

HIV and Aids in Schools

The Political Economy of Pressure Groups and Miseducation
Barrie Craven, Pauline Dixon, Gordon Stewart & James Tooley
Occasional Paper 121; ISBN 0 255 36522 5
£10.00

The Road to Serfdom

The Reader's Digest *condensed version*
Friedrich A. Hayek
Occasional Paper 122; ISBN 0 255 36530 6
£7.50

Bastiat's *The Law*

Introduction by Norman Barry
Occasional Paper 123; ISBN 0 255 36509 8
£7.50

A Globalist Manifesto for Public Policy

Charles Calomiris
Occasional Paper 124; ISBN 0 255 36525 X
£7.50

Euthanasia for Death Duties

Putting Inheritance Tax Out of Its Misery
Barry Bracewell-Milnes
Research Monograph 54; ISBN 0 255 36513 6
£10.00

Liberating the Land
The Case for Private Land-use Planning
Mark Pennington
Hobart Paper 143; ISBN 0 255 36508 x
£10.00

IEA Yearbook of Government Performance 2002/2003
Edited by Peter Warburton
Yearbook 1; ISBN 0 255 36532 2
£15.00

Britain's Relative Economic Performance, 1870–1999
Nicholas Crafts
Research Monograph 55; ISBN 0 255 36524 1
£10.00

Should We Have Faith in Central Banks?
Otmar Issing
Occasional Paper 125; ISBN 0 255 36528 4
£7.50

The Dilemma of Democracy

Arthur Seldon

Hobart Paper 136 (reissue); ISBN 0 255 36536 5

£10.00

Capital Controls: a 'Cure' Worse Than the Problem?

Forrest Capie

Research Monograph 56; ISBN 0 255 36506 3

£10.00

The Poverty of 'Development Economics'

Deepak Lal

Hobart Paper 144 (reissue); ISBN 0 255 36519 5

£15.00

Should Britain Join the Euro?

The Chancellor's Five Tests Examined

Patrick Minford

Occasional Paper 126; ISBN 0 255 36527 6

£7.50

Post-Communist Transition: Some Lessons

Leszek Balcerowicz

Occasional Paper 127; ISBN 0 255 36533 0

£7.50

A Tribute to Peter Bauer

John Blundell et al.

Occasional Paper 128; ISBN 0 255 36531 4

£10.00

Employment Tribunals

Their Growth and the Case for Radical Reform

J. R. Shackleton

Hobart Paper 145; ISBN 0 255 36515 2

£10.00

Fifty Economic Fallacies Exposed

Geoffrey E. Wood

Occasional Paper 129; ISBN 0 255 36518 7

£12.50

A Market in Airport Slots

Keith Boyfield (editor), David Starkie, Tom Bass & Barry Humphreys

Readings 56; ISBN 0 255 36505 5

£10.00

Money, Inflation and the Constitutional Position of the Central Bank

Milton Friedman & Charles A. E. Goodhart

Readings 57; ISBN 0 255 36538 1

£10.00

Corporate Governance: Accountability in the Marketplace

Elaine Sternberg
Second edition
Hobart Paper 147; ISBN 0 255 36542 X
£12.50

The Land Use Planning System

Evaluating Options for Reform
John Corkindale
Hobart Paper 148; ISBN 0 255 36550 0
£10.00

To order copies of currently available IEA papers, or to enquire about availability, please contact:

Lavis Marketing
IEA orders
FREEPOST LON21280
Oxford OX3 7BR

Tel: 01865 767575
Fax: 01865 750079
Email: orders@lavismarketing.co.uk

The IEA also offers a subscription service to its publications. For a single annual payment, currently £40.00 in the UK, you will receive every title the IEA publishes across the course of a year, invitations to events, and discounts on our extensive back catalogue. For more information, please contact:

Subscriptions
The Institute of Economic Affairs
2 Lord North Street
London SW1P 3LB

Tel: 020 7799 8900
Fax: 020 7799 2137
Website: www.iea.org.uk